squeezed

250 juices + smoothies

Published by Murdoch Books Pty Limited.

Murdoch Books Australia
Pier 8/9, 23 Hickson Road, Millers Point NSW 2000
Phone: +61 (0)2 8220 2000 Fax: +61 (0)2 8220 2558

Murdoch Books Ltd UK
Erico House, 6th Floor North, 93–99 Upper Richmond Road
Putney, London SW15 2TG
Phone: + 44 (0) 20 8785 5995 Fax: + 44 (0) 20 8785 5985

Chief Executive: Juliet Rogers
Publisher: Kay Scarlett

Concept and art direction: Marylouise Brammer
Project manager and introduction text: Margaret Malone
Photographer: Tim Robinson
Creative consultant and stylist: Marcus Hay
Recipes by: Jane Lawson and the Murdoch Books Test Kitchen
Recipe introductions by: Francesca Newby
Text editor: Justine Harding
Food preparation: Wendy Quisumbing
Editorial Director: Diana Hill
Production: Monika Vidovic
Stylist's assistants: Tamara Boon and Ashisha Cunningham

National Library of Australia Cataloguing-in-Publication Data
Squeezed
Includes index. ISBN 1 74045 444 8.
1. Fruit juices. 2. Smoothies (Beverages)
641.875

Printed by Midas Printing International in China. First printed in 2004. Reprinted in 2004 and 2005.

IMPORTANT: Those who might be at risk from the effects of salmonella poisoning (the elderly, pregnant women, young children and those suffering from immune deficiency diseases) should consult their doctor with any concerns about eating raw eggs.

The Publisher and stylist would like to thank Breville Pty Ltd for loaning superb equipment for use and for photography. They can be found at www.breville.com.au. Thanks also to the following companies for supplying furniture, props and kitchenware: David Edmonds, Design Mode International, Dinosaur Designs, Jurass, Mitchell & Helen English, Mix (d), Mud Australia, Orson & Blake, (Napery) Sara DeNardi for Feast, Top 3 by Design, and Wheel & Barrow. Special thanks go to the following companies: Chee Soon & Fitzgerald, Cloth, and Signature Prints for fabric and wallpaper backgrounds; Pazotti Tiles, and Bisanna Tiles for tiled backgrounds; Paint for background supplied by Porter's Paints; Jonathan Ingram at InDestudio for custom-made cabinets; Flying Standard for models' clothing; ECC Lighting & Living, FY2K, Spence and Lyda, and Orson & Blake for furniture. Finally, warm thanks to our models: Tamara, Tasman, Brandon and Kaitlin.

squeezed

250 juices + smoothies

Photography by Tim Robinson
Styling by Marcus Hay

MURDOCH BOOKS

contents

squeeze it When life has run you ragged, and even when it hasn't, there is a place close by where help can be found. Let the kitchen be more than just a nod to necessary sustenance — make it shine with

some mighty fine juice concoctions. All you need are some fresh fruit and vegetables, a juicer or blender and a little inspiration, and you'll soon have a whole lot of healing going on.

squeeze it

Many people make fresh juices at home as a way to look after their health. And with very good reason — a glass of fresh fruit or vegetable juice is an excellent way to get a little nutrition into one's system. Fresh juices can repair, protect, energize and improve — not just the body, but the mind and spirit as well. These are serious benefits. However, other people make their own juices because they taste good. This is also very valid: juices are delicious. As well, they are convenient, cheap and easy to make. Anyone can make them, without needing fancy equipment or culinary skills.

But more than health ... more than nutritional balance ... more than even the time-saving benefits of a cleansing breakfast in a glass ... the reason people really squeeze, juice and blend every day across the nation is because we're all budding scientists and artists at heart. Juicing allows you to bring your own creative interpretation to nature's bounty, to bring some order to the chaos of the fruit bowl and a little sense to the vegetables. Juicing lets us take A + B and make C. What's more, there's lots of noise, and things splash about, and different sizes and shapes go in, and liquid comes out, and it may be slushy or smooth or frothy and thick, and is sometimes sunset pink, but other times deep crimson or vivid green — and we're the ones controlling the whole thing. Miraculous!

There are few times in life when you can give free rein to your inner kitchen artist, and feel safe in the knowledge that the results will rarely be less than excellent or beneficial. What could be better?

the good juice

The health benefits associated with regularly drinking fresh fruit and vegetable juices are many and of long standing. We're not talking about some new-fangled fad here. But, equally, there's no time better than the present to repeat them. Juices provide energy to the energy-deficient, protect the immune system, have cleansing and settling properties, give encouragement to a flagging libido, and even make it a bit easier to get going in the morning. Fresh fruit and vegetables contain an amazing array of vitamins, minerals and other trace elements that are known to be essential for good health, and digesting them in liquid form is one of the best ways to help them on their beneficial way. No commercially-prepared juice is going to have the same fresh goodness as your own drink will. The following is a taste of the good things juices contain:

antioxidants are powerful protective substances that neutralize potentially harmful molecules found in the body. These molecules, known as free radicals, are normal by-products of metabolism, but factors such as stress, smoking and pollution can boost their numbers. If left unchecked, free radicals may play a role in the onset of heart disease, osteoporosis and cancer. Some key antioxidants are vitamin E (wheat germ, spinach, avocado), vitamin C (citrus and tropical fruits, green vegetables, berries); and beta-carotene (apricots, dark leafy greens, mangoes, tomatoes, watercress).

minerals The body can't make minerals but it sure does need them. They are present in the body in small amounts, and are essential for numerous jobs ranging from regulating blood pressure to keeping teeth strong and healthy. All of the seven major minerals and nine of the various trace elements are vital to good health. Found in rich supply in fresh juices are minerals such as calcium (dairy, figs and fortified soy products); iron (dried apricots, green leafy vegetables, spinach, nuts); magnesium (nuts, especially almonds); potassium (bananas, dried fruits, tea) and zinc (eggs).

phytochemicals are compounds found naturally in plants. They do not have a nutritional value but are thought to be needed by the body for disease prevention. 'Thought to be' because they're secretive little critters, but ongoing research suggests that phytochemicals can lower the risk of osteoporosis, cancer and inflammatory disorders. The only way to guarantee you get enough phytochemicals is by eating and drinking a wide variety of different coloured fruit and vegetables of the best possible quality.

You may well ask what vitamins aren't needed for: they are vital to fundamental processes such as growth, reproduction and tissue repair; are essential for the normal functioning of every organ in the body; and are also needed to release the energy from dietary carbohydrate, fat, protein and alcohol. Like minerals, most vitamins cannot be made in the body, so must be supplied by the diet. The following vitamins are found in good amounts in fruit and vegetables: the B vitamins (bananas, dried fruits, soy products, wheat germ); vitamin C (citrus fruits, green vegetables, berries, tomatoes, some tropical fruit); and vitamin E (wheat germ, spinach, avocado, nuts).

Who would have thought that fruit and vegetables were so well equipped to fight the good fight? But they are, and so much the better for us.

the juice on juicers

Most juices and smoothies are made with one of two pieces of equipment — a juicer or a blender. Some recipes require both; others also involve the use of a citrus press. But that's about it.

There is no question that the best juicers are expensive and, for most of us, the hardest part about making fresh juices at home is the initial decision to buy the thing. That, and working out where to put it. When choosing a juicer, prices and reliability pretty much go hand in hand upwards, but here are a few things to consider before you buy: does the juicer have parts that are dishwasher proof; what is the motor's size; how easy will it be to clean; how wide is the chute (will it be able to cope with whole fruit and vegetables); does it have low and high speeds; and is there a slide-in froth separator (which is about as good as it gets)? The more expensive juicers generally do work better, and last longer. They also extract more juice per fruit so you get more for your money. **juicers work** by a process of centrifugal motion, spinning the fruit or vegetable pieces in a filter basket fitted with a rotating cutting disk, thus separating the juice from the pulp. The juice comes out the spout; the leftover pulp goes into its own disposal container. A few things to remember: always use the plunger to push food down the chute, not your fingers; use the plunger slowly (this will ensure the greatest amount of juice is extracted from the pulp, and will ease the strain on the filter basket and motor); and put the juice jug or a glass under the spout before turning on. If you wish, line the pulp-collecting container with a plastic bag, as that can be easily discarded later. Do not let the pulp-collecting container overfill. Fruit and vegetables with a high water content, like tomatoes and watermelon, should be juiced on the slower speed (if your machine has this option); and hard ingredients such as carrots, apples, beetroot and fennel work best on a higher speed. All juicers need cleaning. Sad but true. A few tips: always ensure the stainless steel filter is thoroughly clean before use. This means cleaning it properly immediately *after* each use. Once pulp dries on the filter, it will clog the pores and is a bore to remove. Watch fingers when cleaning the filter basket. Some juicers come with a special brush for washing the basket — use it. It will help.

As their name suggests, blenders mix and whizz ingredients to a smooth consistency. Look for ones that can cope with crushed ice cubes. Capacity

varies but the best are the stand alone ones, as they produce smoother drinks. But, really, any blender will do. Chop ingredients such as orchard fruits and bananas finely for best results. Blending ingredients such as plums will give drinks flecked with the skin.

The citrus press is an old stalwart. Be it a simple plastic job, a wooden reamer or a top-of-the-range chrome citrus press with handle, the process is pretty much the same. Take citrus, cut in half, place against citrus press, squeeze and twist. Strain the juice of pips if you wish, before drinking or combining with another juice. Always reliable, a citrus press is time efficient and easy to clean. If you don't have a citrus press, however, just peel the fruit (leaving as much white pith as possible), chop into chunks and pass through a juicer or blender.

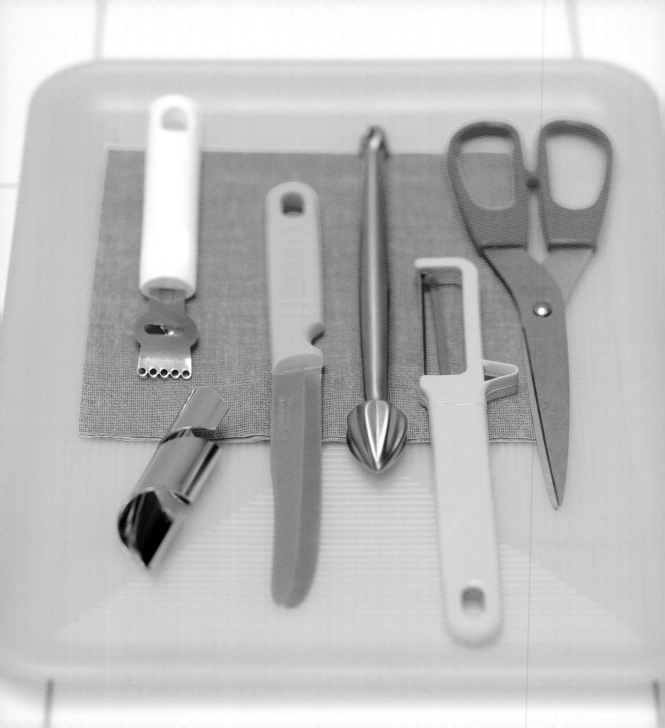

getting a grip

There is not much that can go really wrong when squeezing, blending and whizzing your own fresh juices. But there are a few ways to guarantee great drinks every time. Always use good-quality ingredients — there is nothing to mask their flavours, after all. Use organic where possible, and refrain from using ingredients until they are fully ripe. Use fruit and vegetables straight from the refrigerator, so that the end result is perfectly chilled. If you freeze fruit, such as berries, cherries, chopped mango and overripe banana, use the fruit within two weeks. After that, the flavour fades. Unless otherwise stated, juice fruit and vegetables with the skin on. Remove all pits and hard stones before using. The seeds can stay if juicing but remove if blending. Wash produce before use, scrubbing tough-skinned varieties with a soft brush. Chop ingredients only when you are ready to chuck the pieces in the juicer or blender; otherwise you will cause unnecessary vitamin loss. Don't be shy — experiment, embellish, revise or adapt recipes to find your preferred flavour combinations. It's part of the pleasure. Adjust the consistency of drinks by adding water or still mineral water for a thinner drink, or frozen fruit, crushed ice or frozen yoghurt for a thicker one. Sweeten juices by adding a dash of honey, maple syrup or some ripe banana (though this will affect the drink's consistency). If adding sugar, always use caster (superfine) sugar as it dissolves easily. Experimentation will reveal if you like drinks rich and heavy, with ingredients such as bananas, or clean and sharp, with flavours like citrus and ginger. On the whole, fruit and veg don't mix. Of course, now that you've read that, the first recipe you see will be a **fruit and veg combo**. Give it a go. When juicing fresh herbs or small quantities of ingredients such as a piece of ginger or alfalfa sprouts bunch them together or send them through the juicer alternating with a main ingredient. Whole ice cubes can be added to the blender, but crushing them first gives a better result. There is also **something therapeutic** about smashing tea-towel-wrapped ice cubes against the kitchen bench or hitting them with a rolling pin. It's all part of the fun. Finally, drink juices immediately. If you wait, things start separating, colours change, nutritional value fades and the flavour goes all wrong. This is especially true of juices containing apple and pear, which oxidize quickly. There is no time like the present with fresh juices …

berries'n'cherries   Berries (and cherries and grapes), what words can describe thee? Bold, bright, bounteous (for some of the year), brazen yet blessed, beautiful, beneficial, bodacious and so berry berry beloved. (Little bundles of bursting brilliancy.) Such are these small, juicy fruit, appearing in their best purples and reds every spring and summer. Behold the berry! (And cherries and grapes.) Get into them.

Plump blackberries have a sweet, juicy flavour all their own. They are best used within 2 days of purchasing, or frozen for later use. blackcurrants bring a tartness to drinks that isn't suggested by their size. They are generally used in juice form, often mixed with other fruit juices. Sweet blueberries appear in late spring and are also available frozen. Little powerhouses, they are a fantastic source of antioxidants. Choose firm, plump berries and use within 1 week of buying. cherries need pitting before use. Use a cherry pitter or cut in half and remove the pit with your fingers. It's not that hard. Use fresh cherries within 1 week of buying, otherwise buy frozen, pitted cherries. Fresh cranberries are rare creatures — use dried cranberries or cranberry juice instead. Potassium-rich, naturally sweet grapes are excellent for balancing other stronger flavours. They ripen quickly at room temperature so are best stored in the refrigerator. Wash well to remove any insecticide. Buy fully ripe raspberries on the day they are to be eaten and avoid washing them, or wash them just before using, and handle them as little as possible. What raspberries lack in juice they more than offer in intense colour and flavour. Sieve the juice after blending, if liked. Freeze when in season and buy frozen, unsweetened ones when not. Choose strawberries that are plump, glossy, unbruised and firm and store in the refrigerator for up to 3 days. Wash and hull just before using. Use in the juicer or blender.

It's sweet, it's rich and it's full of what you need.

What's not to fall for?

blueberry crush

150 g (5½ oz) blueberries
750 ml (3 cups) apple and blackcurrant juice
500 ml (2 cups) soda water
1 tablespoon caster (superfine) sugar
ice cubes, to serve

Blend the blueberries, apple and blackcurrant juice, soda water and sugar in a blender until smooth. Serve over ice. Makes 4 medium glasses.

Note: To make a slushy, add the ice cubes, crushed, to the blender when mixing the other ingredients.

Guaranteed not to leave you standing alone.

blue moon

300 g (10½ oz) blueberries
6 small peaches, stones removed
2 cm (¾ inch) piece ginger
pinch ground cinnamon
honey, to taste, optional
ice cubes, to serve

Juice the blueberries, peaches and ginger through a juice extractor. Stir through the cinnamon and honey, if desired, and serve over ice. Makes 2 small glasses.

Mix cherries with berries for a sensory overload, and let the apples add a note of calm.

berries and cherries

150 g (5½ oz) blueberries
200 g (7 oz) cherries, pitted
6 apples, stalks removed
ice cubes, to serve

Juice the blueberries, cherries and apples through a juice extractor. Stir to combine and serve over ice. Makes 2 medium glasses.

Put on the Barry White, slip into a long cool stretch of black velvet and get in the mood for some lurve.

black velvet

500 g (1 lb 2 oz) black seedless grapes
300 g (10^1/$_2$ oz) blackberries
400 g (14 oz) cherries, pitted
ice cubes, to serve

Juice the grapes, blackberries and cherries through a juice extractor. Stir to combine and serve over ice. Makes 2 small glasses.

Note: This juice is very rich and sweet so only a small amount is needed. You can top it up with soda water to make 4 tall glasses.

blue moon

Complex and sophisticated, the sweet fruit is mellowed by the deep bass notes of cold black tea.

cherry and berry punch

400 g (14 oz) cherries, pitted
200 g (7 oz) blackberries
200 g (7 oz) blueberries
125 g (4$\frac{1}{2}$ oz) strawberries, hulled and halved
750 ml (3 cups) dry ginger ale
500 ml (2 cups) lemonade
250 ml (1 cup) cold black tea
zest of 1 lemon, cut into long thin strips
10 mint leaves, torn
ice cubes, to serve

Put the cherries, blackberries, blueberries, strawberries, dry ginger ale, lemonade, tea, lemon zest and mint into a jug. Cover the jug and chill for at least 3 hours. Add ice cubes to serve. Makes 10 small glasses.

Serve with sushi on a Friday night and say sayonara baby to the working week.

cherry blossom slushy

3 large Nashi pears, stalks removed
300 g (10½ oz) frozen pitted cherries
8–10 ice cubes, crushed

Juice the Nashi through a juice extractor. Add the Nashi juice, frozen cherries and ice cubes to a blender and process until smooth. Makes 2 medium glasses.

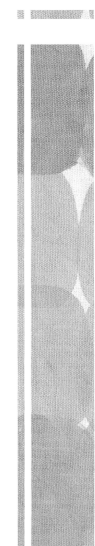

Life's a bowl of cherries so juice them up and forget about the pits.

cherry, black grape and apple juice

400 g (14 oz) cherries, pitted
500 g (1 lb 2 oz) black or green seedless grapes
6 apples, stalks removed
250 ml (1 cup) cranberry juice
ice cubes, to serve

Juice the cherries, grapes and apples through a juice extractor. Stir through the cranberry juice and serve over ice. Makes 2 large glasses.

Pour over vanilla ice cream for a sumptuous dessert.

cherry syrup

1.5 kg (3 lb 5 oz) cherries, pitted
4 strips of lemon zest
juice of 1 lemon
230 g (1 cup) caster (superfine) sugar

Combine the cherries, lemon zest, lemon juice, sugar and 500 ml (2 cups) water in a large saucepan. Bring to the boil and cook for 30 minutes, occasionally pressing on the cherries with a potato masher to release their juice. Strain through a fine sieve, pressing on the solids, then strain again into a very clean glass jar or bottle and seal. Refrigerate for up to 2 weeks. Makes 500 ml (2 cups).

Note: To serve, pour a little syrup into a glass and top with soda water and a twist of lime. Also great in cocktails or in coconut milk with a dash of chocolate syrup over lots of ice. Delicious over ice cream too.

cherry blossom slushy

Go ape for the grape and get some serious antioxidant action.

grape ape!

500 g (1 lb 2 oz) red grapes
10 apricots, stones removed
4 pears, stalks removed
3 apples, stalks removed

Juice the grapes, apricots, pears and apples through a juice extractor. Stir
to combine. Makes 2 large glasses.

42

When the spirit is willing but the body a little sluggish, let naturally sweet grapes give you the boost you need.

red grape and rockmelon juice

500 g (1 lb 2 oz) red seedless grapes
1 rockmelon (or other orange-fleshed melon), peeled,
  seeded and chopped
2 cm (3/4 inch) piece ginger

Juice the grapes, rockmelon and ginger through a juice extractor. Stir to combine. Makes 2 medium glasses.

Good things begin with g — gemstones, girls and grape'n'guava.

grape'n'guava

500 g (1 lb 2 oz) green or black seedless grapes
2 cm (3/4 inch) piece ginger
1 lime, peeled
4 large passionfruit
375 ml (1 1/2 cups) guava juice
ice cubes, to serve

Juice the grapes, ginger and lime through a juice extractor. Strain the passionfruit pulp well, discarding the seeds. Combine the passionfruit juice with the grape mixture and guava juice. Serve over ice cubes. Makes 2 medium glasses.

When you're melting under the summer sun, reverse the trend with this cool concoction.

zippy grape and apple juice

500 g (1 lb 2 oz) green seedless grapes
6 apples, stalks removed
1 lemon, peeled
ice cubes, to serve

Juice the grapes, apples and lemon through a juice extractor. Stir to combine and serve over ice. Makes 2 medium glasses.

Note: Freeze the juice in ice-block trays for a refreshing treat.

red grape and rockmelon juice

Choose a sweet, mellow golden apple variety that will let the raspberries shine.

raspapple freezie

6 apples, stalks removed or 500 ml (2 cups) apple juice
300 g (10 1/2 oz) frozen raspberries

Juice the apples through a juice extractor. Blend the apple juice and frozen raspberries in a blender until smooth. Makes 2 large glasses.

All work and no play is never a good idea — this drink helps factor in a little r'n'r.

r'n'r

300 g (10½ oz) frozen raspberries
juice of 1 lime
½ rockmelon (or other orange-fleshed melon), peeled,
  seeded and chopped
1 teaspoon honey

Blend the frozen raspberries with the lime juice in a blender in short bursts until the berries are starting to break up. Add a little water if necessary to help blend the berries. Add the rockmelon and honey and blend until smooth. Makes 2 medium glasses.

Like a ruby red stiletto, this is a sharp and sophisticated drop.

raspberry, pear and grape juice

250 g (9 oz) raspberries
4 pears, stalks removed
500 g (1 lb 2 oz) green grapes
ice cubes, to serve

Juice the raspberries, pears and grapes through a juice extractor. Stir to combine and serve over ice. Makes 2 large glasses.

The tart sweetness of Granny Smiths blends in perfect
harmony with the sweet richness of raspberries.

raspberry and apple juice

150 g (5¹/₂ oz) raspberries
6 Granny Smith apples, stalks removed
ice cubes, to serve
mint sprigs, to garnish

Juice the raspberries and apples through a juice extractor. Pour into a jug
and chill. Stir to combine and serve over ice, garnished with mint sprigs.
Makes 2 medium glasses.

r'n'r

Apple, berry, cherry … let's start at the very beginning, the very best place to start! It's an elementary choice, really.

abc

150 g (5½ oz) raspberries
400 g (14 oz) cherries, pitted
6 apples, stalks removed
ice cubes, to serve

Juice the raspberries, cherries and apples through a juice extractor. Stir to combine and serve over ice. Makes 2 large glasses.

This pink tonic is just the ticket for a lazy afternoon game of tennis with the chaps.

raspberry lemonade

300 g (10½ oz) raspberries
275 g (1¼ cups) sugar
500 ml (2 cups) lemon juice
ice cubes, to serve
mint leaves, to garnish

Blend the raspberries and sugar in a blender until smooth. Push the mixture through a strong sieve and discard the seeds. Add the lemon juice, mix well and pour into a large jug. Stir through 1.5 litres (6 cups) water and chill well. Serve over ice, garnished with mint leaves. Makes 6 medium glasses.

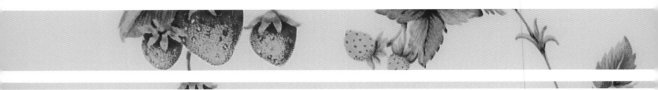

This bird won't give you wings but it will help ground your immune system.

strange bird

500 g (1 lb 2 oz) strawberries, hulled
6 kiwifruit, peeled
ice cubes, to serve

Juice the strawberries and kiwifruit through a juice extractor. Stir to combine and serve over ice. Makes 2 small glasses.

Ramp up the passion factor with a zinger of a juice — serve
just before bed!

strawberry, rockmelon and passionfruit juice

500 g (1 lb 2 oz) strawberries, hulled
1 small rockmelon (or other orange-fleshed melon), peeled,
   seeded and chopped
2 large passionfruit

Juice the strawberries and rockmelon through a juice extractor. Stir
through the passionfruit pulp. Makes 2 medium glasses.

strange bird

Haven't you heard? Rhubarb is the sweetest vege in town.

strawberry and rhubarb lemonade

500 g (1 lb 2 oz) strawberries, hulled and halved
800 g (1 lb 12 oz) rhubarb, chopped
230 g (1 cup) caster (superfine) sugar
1 large mint sprig
125 ml (1/2 cup) lemon juice
ice cubes, to serve
small mint sprigs, to garnish

Combine the strawberries, rhubarb, sugar, mint and lemon juice in a large saucepan and add 1.5 litres (6 cups) water. Bring to the boil over high heat, then reduce to a simmer and cook for 15 minutes. Remove from the heat and allow to cool. Strain through a fine sieve, pressing on the solids. Strain again into a jug and chill well. Serve over ice with a small sprig of mint in a glass. Makes 4 medium glasses.

Note: Half fill a glass with strawberry and rhubarb lemonade and top up with soda water for another refreshing drink.

Buff up for the beach with a nutrient-heavy de-tox draught.

summer de-tox

2 peaches
3 oranges, peeled
250 g (9 oz) strawberries, hulled
300 g (10½ oz) red seedless grapes

Cut a cross in the base of the peaches. Put them in a heatproof bowl and cover with boiling water. Leave for 1–2 minutes, then remove with a slotted spoon and plunge into cold water. Remove the skin and stones, and chop the flesh. Juice the oranges, strawberries, grapes and peaches through a juice extractor. Stir to combine and serve with long spoons. Makes 2 medium glasses.

Let the season guide your footsteps — choose whatever fresh berries are available.

mixed berry and lemonade fizz

100 g (3 1/2 oz) strawberries, hulled
50 g (1 3/4 oz) blueberries
750 ml (3 cups) lemonade
2 scoops lemon sorbet

Blend the strawberries, blueberries, lemonade and lemon sorbet in a blender until well combined. Pour into glasses and add any extra berries, if desired. Makes 4 small glasses.

A creamy cloud of fruity heaven, perfect for drifting along on a sunny afternoon.

strawberry, kiwi and peach slushy

250 g (9 oz) strawberries, hulled
2 kiwifruit, peeled and chopped
200 g (7 oz) canned peaches in natural juice
3 scoops orange sorbet or gelato

Blend the strawberries, kiwifruit, undrained peaches and sorbet or gelato in a blender until smooth. Makes 2 large glasses.

mixed berry and lemonade fizz

orchard fruits When apricots first came along, all things round, soft and bottom-like sat up and took notice. When peaches came along, blossoms and downy creatures took heart, while pears gave shape to

artist's dreams, apples helped pies find their form and plums plumbed new depths. When things look glum, turn to orchard fruit. It's hard to remain down when faced with a soft, round, furry, yummy thing.

apples are ideally suited to juicing and blending: they need only washing, their stalk removed, and then cut into rough chunks before tossing into the chosen machine. They leave little mess when used in a juicer, and give a clear, cleansing drink. Avoid floury apples. Canned apples are good for blending. Velvety, ripe apricots are best used on the day of purchase. Remove the stones before juicing or blending. Canned apricots in natural juice and apricot nectar are both ideal for blending; dried apricots are suitable for infusions. Smooth-skinned nectarines are great in the juicer or blender. No need to peel but do remove the stone. The skin may fleck blended drinks. The same goes for peaches; juice or blend these babies. The height of summer is the time to indulge in peaches — this is when their flavour is at their fragrant, juicy best. Again, no need to peel, just remove the stone. Canned peaches can be blended. When juicing, pears need their stalks removed but everything else, cores and seeds, can stay. Peel and core when blending. Use pears that are just short of fully ripe — you want the natural sweetness that comes with ripening but with a little crunch to make juicing easier. Pear (and apple) juice discolours quickly, so add citrus juice and drink immediately. Nashi pears can be treated like apples. The best plums are pleasantly scented, yield slightly when pressed and have a whitish bloom on the skin. Stone, then use in a juicer or blender. Prunes are dried plums — use them pitted.

Make this in the mellow months of autumn, when the orchards are heavy with sun-ripened fruit.

minted apple orchard

6 apples, stalks removed
3 pears, stalks removed
20 g (1 cup) mint leaves, plus extra to garnish

Juice the apples, pears and mint leaves through a juice extractor. Stir to combine and drink straight away. Garnish with a sprig of mint if desired. Makes 2 large glasses.

Don't just grapple with a cold, tackle it to the ground with this vitamin-C-rich apple and zucchini drink.

zapple

6 apples, stalks removed
2 zucchini (courgette)
3 cm (1¼ inch) piece ginger
ice cubes, to serve

Juice the apples, zucchini and ginger through a juice extractor. Stir to combine and serve over ice. Makes 2 large glasses.

Jazz up this gentle duo with a full-on blast of ginger spice.

apple, celery and ginger juice

9 apples, stalks removed
9 celery stalks
3 cm (1¼ inch) piece ginger

Juice the apples, celery and ginger through a juice extractor. Stir to combine. Makes 2 large glasses.

A shot of this green magic will get you through a grey day.

apple, celery, cucumber and basil juice

9 apples, stalks removed
6 celery stalks
1 large cucumber
7 g (¼ cup) basil leaves

Juice the apples, celery, cucumber and basil through a juice extractor. Stir to combine. Makes 2 large glasses.

minted apple orchard

No-one can be sweet all the time — celebrate the sharper side of life.

apple and cranberry infusion

200 g (2²/₃ cups) dried apple
170 g (1¹/₂ cups) dried cranberries
zest of 1 lemon
55 g (¹/₄ cup) caster (superfine) sugar
ice cubes, to serve
fresh apple slices, to garnish

Combine the dried apple, dried cranberries, lemon zest and sugar in a large saucepan and add 4 litres (16 cups) water. Stir over high heat until the sugar has dissolved. Bring to the boil, then reduce the heat and simmer for 35 minutes. Remove from the heat and allow to cool. Strain and chill well. Serve over ice, garnished with a thin slice of fresh apple. Makes 8 medium glasses.

Note: Serve the leftover strained fruit with ice cream or use it for a pie or pastry filling.

Revisit your cider-fuelled student years without the grungy flat mates tagging along for the ride.

apple fizz

6 apples, stalks removed
1 lemon, peeled
250 ml (1 cup) apple cider
ice cubes, to serve

Juice the apples and lemon through a juice extractor. Stir through the apple cider and serve over ice. Makes 2 large glasses.

Juice in bulk and fill your best bowl — your guests will be pleased as punch.

apricot fruit spritzer

500 ml (2 cups) apricot nectar
250 ml (1 cup) apple juice
250 ml (1 cup) orange juice
500 ml (2 cups) soda water
8 ice cubes

Put the apricot nectar, apple juice, orange juice, soda water and ice cubes into a large jug and stir to combine. Makes 4 medium glasses.

Everyone knows apricots look like cute little bottoms. They're also very good for you. Grab them while you can.

apricot, orange and ginger juice

10 apricots, stones removed
6 oranges, peeled
3 cm (1¼ inch) piece ginger
ice cubes, to serve

Juice the apricots, oranges and ginger through a juice extractor. Stir to combine and serve over ice. Makes 2 large glasses.

apricot fruit spritzer

A sweet combination that's picture perfect for a couple of sweethearts to share.

nectarine, grape and strawberry juice

6 nectarines, stones removed
500 g (1 lb 2 oz) green grapes
250 g (9 oz) strawberries, hulled
ice cubes, to serve

Juice the nectarines, grapes and strawberries through a juice extractor. Stir to combine and serve over ice. Makes 2 large glasses.

Pungent basil leaves bring out the delicate sweetness of fresh ripe nectarines.

nectarine and basil juice

4 nectarines, stones removed
15 g (1/2 cup) basil leaves
4 oranges, peeled

Juice the nectarines, basil and oranges through a juice extractor. Stir to combine. Makes 2 medium glasses.

Let exquisitely perfumed lychees clear out the cobwebs from a fuzzy morning head.

perfumed nectarine

6 large nectarines, stones removed
4 peaches, stones removed
250 g (9 oz) lychees, peeled and seeded

Juice the nectarines, peaches and lychees through a juice extractor. Save a thin slice of nectarine for garnishing, if desired. Stir to combine. Makes 2 large glasses.

Sit back and watch the world go by with a glass of this sweet, subtle nectar.

nectar of the gods

6 nectarines, stones removed
125 ml (1/2 cup) apple juice
1/2 teaspoon natural vanilla extract (essence)
1/2 teaspoon rosewater
ice cubes, to serve

Juice the nectarines through a juice extractor. Stir through the apple juice, vanilla and rosewater and serve over ice. Makes 2 small glasses.

perfumed nectarine

The sweetest member of the rose family, peaches bring a flush of unadulterated good health to the cheeks.

peach, kiwi and apple juice

4 peaches, stones removed
6 kiwifruit, peeled
3 apples, stalks removed

Juice the peaches, kiwifruit and apples through a juice extractor. Stir to combine. Makes 2 large glasses.

Like a southern belle with a headache, this is a smooth number with bite.

spiky peach

8 peaches, stones removed
1 small pineapple, peeled
10 g (1/2 cup) mint leaves
2 cm (3/4 inch) piece ginger

Juice the peaches, pineapple, mint and ginger through a juice extractor. Stir to combine. Makes 2 large glasses.

Thick and smooth, this drink gives the mind and body a gentle nudge into the new day.

peach and rockmelon juice

4 peaches
1/2 rockmelon (or other orange-fleshed melon), peeled,
  seeded and chopped
600 ml (21 fl oz) orange juice
12 ice cubes
1 tablespoon lime juice

Cut a small cross in the base of the peaches. Put them in a heatproof bowl and cover with boiling water. Leave for 1–2 minutes, then remove with a slotted spoon and plunge into cold water. Remove the skin and stones, and chop the flesh into bite-size pieces. Blend the peaches, rockmelon, orange juice and ice cubes in a blender until smooth. If the juice is too thick, add a little iced water. Stir through the lime juice. Makes 2 large glasses.

Add a little heat to sun-warmed peaches with a pinch of freshly grated nutmeg.

fuzzy peach

6 peaches, stones removed
1 lemon, peeled
large pinch freshly grated nutmeg
250 ml (1 cup) dry ginger ale
ice cubes, to serve

Juice the peaches and lemon through a juice extractor. Stir through the nutmeg and dry ginger ale. Serve over ice. Makes 2 large glasses.

fuzzy peach

An apple a day keeps the doctor away ... so double up and get ahead.

pear, apple and ginger juice

3 pears, stalks removed
5 Granny Smith apples, stalks removed
3 cm (1¼ inch) piece ginger

Juice the pear, apple and ginger through a juice extractor. Stir to combine.
Makes 2 medium glasses.

This gorgeous juice is subtle and simple.

blushing nashi

6 Nashi pears, stalks removed
250 g (9 oz) strawberries, hulled
3 cm (1¼ inch) piece ginger

Juice the pears, strawberries and ginger through a juice extractor. Stir to combine. Makes 2 large glasses.

Note: Use pears that are just ripe, but not overripe, otherwise they won't juice well.

Mint leaves plucked fresh from the plant is one of life's surest pick-me-ups.

pear and mint frappé

4 pears, peeled, cored and chopped
2 teaspoons roughly chopped mint
3 teaspoons caster (superfine) sugar
10 ice cubes
mint leaves, to garnish

Blend the pears, mint and sugar in a blender until smooth. Add the ice cubes and blend until smooth. Serve garnished with the extra mint leaves. Makes 2 medium glasses.

Peppermint is well known as a stomach calmer and its fresh aroma can also lift your mood.

pear, melon and peppermint juice

3 pears, stalks removed
1/2 small rockmelon (or other orange-fleshed melon), peeled,
  seeded and chopped
few peppermint leaves
ice cubes, to serve

Juice the pears, rockmelon and peppermint leaves through a juice extractor. Stir to combine and serve over ice. Makes 4 small glasses.

Note: The best way to select a ripe melon is to use your nose — if it has a strong sweet fragrance and thick raised netting you can almost guarantee it is ready to eat.

pear, melon and peppermint juice

If orange juice doesn't do it for you any more, give this a go.

plum, orange and vanilla

10 small plums, stones removed
6 oranges, peeled
1/2 teaspoon natural vanilla extract (essence)
ice cubes, to serve

Juice the plums and oranges through a juice extractor. Stir through the vanilla and serve over ice. Makes 2 large glasses.

Note: Use the ripest plums you can find.

Some days you need calming drinks. Other days you don't.

sweet and spicy plum

10 small plums, stones removed
3 cm (1¼ inch) piece ginger
200 g (7 oz) cherries, pitted
3 oranges, peeled
20 g (1 cup) mint leaves
1 teaspoon honey
ice cubes, to serve

Juice the plums, ginger, cherries, oranges and mint through a juice extractor. Stir through the honey, mixing well, and serve over ice. Makes 2 medium glasses.

Yummy plummy in your tummy keeps you on the go.

plum and basil tango

10 small plums, stones removed
2 limes, peeled
10 g (1/3 cup) basil leaves
375 ml (1 1/2 cups) lemonade
ice cubes, to serve
basil leaves, to garnish, extra

Juice the plums, limes and basil leaves through a juice extractor. Stir through the lemonade. Serve over ice, garnished with basil leaves. Makes 2 large glasses.

One of these once a week and it'll be once a day for you.

regulator

125 g (4½ oz) pitted prunes
honey, to taste, optional
ice cubes, to serve

Blend the prunes with 500 ml (2 cups) cold water in a blender until smooth. Stir through the honey, if desired. Strain and serve over ice. Makes 2 small glasses.

sweet and spicy plum

tropical-à-go-go Heady perfumes, sticky flesh, vibrant colours and bizarre shapes are common occurrences among plant life in the world's torrid zones. For the poor witless juicer (meaning you and I), to meet

tropical fruit on their own terms is to enter into a strange world where one mango is never enough, loved ones turn combatants over the last passionfruit and pith helmuts seem entirely appropriate.

Blenders were probably designed with bananas in mind, even overripe ones. Just peel and chop, and mix with yoghurt, milk or ice cream. Fragrant, slightly acidic, pink or red-fleshed guavas have only a short season, so they mostly grace the juicing world already juiced. If you *are* using the fresh fruit, make sure it is fully ripe, then peel and dice. Small, green and furry, kiwi fruit are rich in vitamin C and potassium. Peel and dice for both juicer and blender. For lovers of mangoes, no effort is too great — cut the flesh over the bowl or blender to catch the drips. Choose fruit that is heavy, with a sweet, rich scent. Some juicers don't mind melon skin, be it honeydew or orange-fleshed melon such as rockmelon, but if in doubt cut the flesh away, deseed and chop. The riper the fruit, the sweeter the juice. Only when a papaya is fully ripe, should you seize the moment. Halve, remove the seeds and scoop out the flesh. Retain the seeds if you want; they are edible. To seed or not to seed passionfruit. To avoid any grittiness, strain the pulp before blending. Not to be confused with papaya, pawpaw is yellow-skinned, sweet and fragrant: ideal for the blender. A giant among juicing fruit, the pineapple makes an excellent base ingredient. Chop finely and remove the eyes if blending. Choose ones that feel heavy for their size and have a strong perfume. All parts of a watermelon are edible — remove the seeds if that takes your fancy, or look out for seedless varieties.

Get your motor running with this energy blast.

banana starter

2 bananas, chopped
100 g (3½ oz) frozen blueberries
1 red apple, cored
300 ml (10½ fl oz) apple juice
2 ice cubes

Blend the banana, frozen blueberries, apple, apple juice and ice cubes in a blender until smooth. Makes 4 small glasses.

Factor in 8 scoops of sorbet — one for the blender, one for me, one for the blender …

banana, kiwi and lemon frappé

2 bananas, chopped
3 kiwifruit, peeled and chopped
4 scoops lemon sorbet

Blend the banana, kiwifruit and sorbet in a blender until smooth. Makes 2 medium glasses.

Drink your way to tropical heaven.

guava, pineapple and pear

1 small pineapple, peeled
4 pears, stalks removed
250 ml (1 cup) guava juice
ice cubes, to serve

Juice the pineapple and pears through a juice extractor. Stir through the guava juice and serve over ice. Makes 2 large glasses.

Note: For a smoother juice, cut out the woody heart of the pineapple.

Pale pink and lime green all of a sudden seem to go so well together.

guava juice and soda with zested lime blocks

zest and juice of 2 limes
2 tablespoons lime juice cordial
500 ml (2 cups) soda water
750 ml (3 cups) guava juice

Put the lime juice, lime cordial and half the soda water into a jug and mix together well. Pour into an ice-cube tray and top each cube with a little of the lime zest. Freeze until solid. Divide the ice cubes among 4 glasses and top with the combined guava juice and remaining soda water. Makes 4 medium glasses.

Note: The colour of guava flesh will vary from pale yellow to soft pink. Look for the pink-fleshed varieties, which tend to be sweeter and have a slightly stronger fragrance.

banana, kiwi and lemon frappé

Gorgeously green with a minty zing, this drink captures a fresh spring morning in a glass.

honeydew, pineapple and mint juice

1 honeydew melon, peeled, seeded and chopped
1 small pineapple, peeled
10 g (1/2 cup) mint leaves

Juice the honeydew, pineapple and mint leaves through a juice extractor. Stir to combine. Makes 2 large glasses.

Lacking passion with your honey? Just prepare this drink, serve and look out.

honeydew melon and passionfruit

1 honeydew melon, peeled, seeded and chopped
6 passionfruit (see Note)
ice cubes, to serve

Juice the honeydew through a juice extractor. Stir through the passionfruit pulp and chill well. Stir to combine and serve in a jug with lots of ice. Makes 2 medium glasses.

Note: You will need about 120 g (4 1/2 oz) passionfruit pulp, which will give approximately 1/2 cup of pulp. If the passionfruit are not particularly juicy, you may need to add some canned passionfruit pulp.

Cool down on a sultry afternoon with a long, deep sip of this chilled little number.

melon freezie

1/3 honeydew melon, peeled, seeded and chopped
1/2 small rockmelon (or other orange-fleshed melon), peeled,
 seeded and chopped
12 ice cubes
500 ml (2 cups) orange juice

Blend the honeydew and rockmelon in a blender for 1 minute, or until smooth. Add the ice cubes and orange juice and blend for a further 30 seconds. Transfer to a large shallow plastic dish and freeze for 3 hours. Return to the blender and blend quickly until smooth. Serve with straws and long spoons. Makes 4 medium glasses.

Note: Roughly break up the ice cubes first by placing them in a clean tea towel and hitting on a hard surface.

Sweet as honey and soft as dew, you know this drink's just right for you.

honeydew punch

¹/₂ honeydew melon, peeled, seeded and chopped
1 green apple, cored
2 oranges, peeled
ice cubes, to serve

Juice the honeydew, apple and orange through a juice extractor. Stir to combine and serve over ice. Makes 2 small glasses.

honeydew, pineapple and mint juice

An excellent antioxidant, turn to this drink when you've been hitting the other grape juice a little too hard.

kiwi, grape and orange juice

6 kiwifruit, peeled
500 g (1 lb 2 oz) green seedless grapes
3 oranges, peeled
1 large passionfruit

Juice the kiwifruit, grapes and oranges through a juice extractor. Stir through the passionfruit pulp. Makes 2 large glasses.

The sweetest and gentlest of the melons, honeydew is the perfect companion to tart and tangy lemon juice.

kiwi, honeydew and lemon juice

6 kiwifruit, peeled
1 honeydew melon, peeled, seeded and chopped
1 lemon, peeled

Juice the kiwifruit, honeydew and lemon through a juice extractor. Stir to combine. Makes 2 medium glasses.

Serve this kiwi charmer to a new mum as a restorative tonic.

kiwi delight

3 kiwifruit, peeled and sliced
80 g (1/2 cup) chopped pineapple
1 banana, chopped
250 ml (1 cup) tropical fruit juice
2 ice cubes

Blend the kiwifruit, pineapple, banana, fruit juice and ice cubes in a blender until smooth. Makes 4 small glasses.

Some star appeal at breakfast and you'll be shining all day long.

star appeal

6 kiwifruit, peeled
4 starfruit (carambola)
1 small pineapple, peeled

Juice the kiwifruit, starfruit and pineapple through a juice extractor. Stir to combine. Makes 2 large glasses.

kiwi delight

Mango juice dribbling down hands and arms is part of the pleasure, but try and get it in the blender.

mango summer haze

2 mangoes, chopped
500 ml (2 cups) orange juice
55 g (¼ cup) caster (superfine) sugar
500 ml (2 cups) sparkling mineral water
ice cubes, to serve
mango slices, to garnish, optional

Blend the mango, orange juice and sugar in a blender until smooth. Stir through the mineral water. Serve over ice and garnish with fresh mango slices, if desired. Makes 6 large glasses.

Mango has never had it so good — cosseted and surrounded by fizzy sweetness.

mango and mandarin chill

1 mango, sliced
500 ml (2 cups) mandarin juice
125 ml (1/2 cup) lime juice cordial
375 ml (1 1/2 cups) soda water
2 tablespoons caster (superfine) sugar
ice cubes, to serve

Freeze the mango for about 1 hour, or until semi-frozen. Combine the mandarin juice, cordial, soda water and sugar in a jug. Put the mango slices and some ice cubes into each glass, then pour in the juice mixture. Makes 2 medium glasses.

Note: For those with a sensitive sweet tooth, add the sugar to taste only at the end.

This thick juice will calm the storm of any upset tummy.

mango, apple and lime

3 mangoes, peeled, stones removed
6 apples, stalks removed
2 limes, peeled
2 cm (3/4 inch) piece ginger
honey, to taste, optional

Juice the mangoes, apples, limes and ginger through a juice extractor. Stir through a little honey, if desired. Makes 2 medium glasses.

It takes two to tango, so try not drink this on your own.

mango tango

2 mangoes, peeled, stones removed
1 small pineapple, peeled
2 panama or large passionfruit
375 ml (1¹/₂ cups) sparkling grape juice

Juice the mangoes and pineapple through a juice extractor. Stir through the passionfruit pulp and grape juice. Makes 2 large glasses.

mango summer haze

Sprinkle some orange nasturtium petals over the glasses and this drink becomes almost too pretty to drink. Almost.

papaya crush with lime sorbet

300 g (10½ oz) chopped red papaya
1–2 tablespoons lime juice
4 scoops lime sorbet
crushed ice
lime zest, to garnish

Blend the papaya, lime juice, 2 scoops of lime sorbet and some crushed ice in a blender until thick and smooth. Pour into 2 tall glasses and top each with a scoop of sorbet. Garnish with lime zest and serve with spoons. Makes 2 large glasses.

For a sunrise special, juice the strawberries separately then stir them through in a loose crimson swirl.

papaya, rockmelon and strawberry juice

1 papaya
1 rockmelon (or other orange-fleshed melon), peeled,
  seeded and chopped
500 g (1 lb 2 oz) strawberries, hulled
2 limes, peeled
ice cubes, to serve

Juice the papaya, rockmelon, strawberries and limes through a juice extractor. Stir to combine and serve over ice. Makes 2 medium glasses.

Aloha summer, here we come.

hawaiian crush

100 g (3½ oz) papaya, peeled, seeded and chopped
200 g (1 cup) chopped watermelon
250 ml (1 cup) apple juice
6 large ice cubes

Blend the papaya, watermelon, apple juice and ice cubes in a blender until smooth. Chill well. Makes 2 medium glasses.

Clean, crisp lychees hook up with earthy passionfruit for an affair worth remembering.

lychee passion fizz

500 g (1 lb 2 oz) lychees, peeled and seeded
2 cm (3/4 inch) piece ginger
3 large passionfruit
500 ml (2 cups) lemonade or soda water

Juice the lychees and ginger through a juice extractor. Stir through the passionfruit pulp and lemonade or soda water. Makes 2 large glasses.

hawaiian crush

Alive with intense flavours, this sweet syrup lifts fizzy water into the realm of the divine.

passionfruit syrup

6 panama or large passionfruit
125 ml (1/2 cup) lemon juice
115 g (1/2 cup) caster (superfine) sugar

Combine the passionfruit pulp, lemon juice, sugar and 500 ml (2 cups) water in a saucepan over high heat. Stir until the sugar has dissolved. Bring to the boil, then reduce to a simmer and cook for 1 1/2 hours or until reduced by half and slightly syrupy. Allow to cool, then strain, pressing on the solids. Pour into a very clean glass jar or bottle and seal. Refrigerate for up to 2 weeks. Makes 375 ml (1 1/2 cups).

Note: To serve, pour a little syrup into a glass with ice and top with soda water, lemonade or dry ginger ale.

The wrinklier the passionfruit, the sweeter the pulp, so get down with an oldie.

passionfruit lime crush

6 panama or large passionfruit
185 ml (3/4 cup) lime juice cordial
750 ml (3 cups) dry ginger ale
crushed ice, to serve

Combine the passionfruit pulp, cordial and dry ginger ale in a large jug and mix together well. Half fill 4 large glasses with crushed ice and add the passionfruit mixture. Makes 4 large glasses.

If it's all been a bit of a blur so far, let this tangy tropical blend set you straight.

morning blended fruit juice

1/2 pineapple, peeled and chopped
1 large pear, stalk removed
1 banana, chopped
40 g (1 1/2 oz) chopped pawpaw
375 ml (1 1/2 cups) orange juice

Blend the pineapple, pear, banana, pawpaw and orange juice in a blender until smooth. Makes 4 medium glasses.

If you're feeling truly indulgent, serve this luscious juice over ice cream for a tropicana fantasy.

tropical fruit frappé

160 g (1 cup) chopped pineapple
¼ small rockmelon (or other orange-fleshed melon), peeled, seeded and chopped
1 banana, chopped
180 g (1 cup) chopped pawpaw
1 mango, chopped
250 ml (1 cup) pineapple juice
crushed ice

Blend the pineapple, rockmelon, banana, pawpaw and mango in a blender until smooth. Add the pineapple juice and crushed ice and blend until the frappé is thick and the ice has thoroughly broken down. Serves 4.

Note: This makes a great breakfast in a glass. The fruit must be ripe or you'll need to add sugar. Add a little coconut milk if you prefer a creamy drink.

passionfruit syrup

The mild green goodness of the kiwifruit gently undercuts the acid kick of the pineapple.

pineapple, kiwi and mint

1/2 small pineapple, peeled
6 kiwifruit, peeled
10 g (1/2 cup) mint leaves
2 cm (3/4 inch) piece ginger

Juice the pineapple, kiwifruit, mint and ginger through a juice extractor. Stir to combine. Makes 2 medium glasses.

This smooth, thick drink has style and substance — it can't help but be good for you.

tropical slurp

1 small pineapple, peeled
3 oranges, peeled
1 large banana, chopped
1 mango, chopped
ice cubes, to serve

Juice the pineapple and oranges through a juice extractor. Transfer to a blender with the banana and mango and blend until smooth. Serve over ice. Makes 2 medium glasses.

Bewitch yourself with this tingly little number.

fresh pineapple juice with mandarin sorbet

1 large pineapple, peeled
250 ml (1 cup) dry ginger ale
4 scoops mandarin sorbet

148

Juice the pineapple through a juice extractor. Combine the pineapple juice and dry ginger ale in a large jug and chill. Stir to combine, pour into 2 glasses and top each with 2 scoops of sorbet. Makes 2 medium glasses.

Sweet yet slightly astringent, this drink can catch you off your guard.

pineapple delight

1/2 pineapple, peeled and chopped
500 ml (2 cups) lemonade
2 tablespoons lime juice
mint leaves, to garnish

Blend the pineapple in a blender for 1–2 minutes, or until as smooth as possible. Pour the lemonade into a jug and stir through the pineapple purée. Add the lime juice and mix well. Serve garnished with mint leaves. Makes 4 small glasses.

fresh pineapple juice with mandarin sorbet

Sometimes only a bit of rough will do.

rough melon

800 g (4 cups) chopped watermelon
1 small pineapple, peeled
500 g (1 lb 2 oz) green seedless grapes

Juice the watermelon, pineapple and grapes through a juice extractor. Stir to combine. Makes 2 large glasses.

Open your eyes to the joy of a long, cool, liquid breakfast.

watermelon breakfast juice

700 g (3$\frac{1}{2}$ cups) chopped watermelon
2 tablespoons lime juice
1–2 cm ($\frac{1}{2}$–$\frac{3}{4}$ inch) piece ginger, grated, to taste
2 tablespoons chopped mint

Blend the watermelon, lime juice, ginger and mint in a blender in short
bursts. (Be careful not to overblend or the mixture will go frothy.) Makes
2 large glasses.

Even endless summers drift to a close — help them linger with
this slow, cool number.

watermelon and kiwi cooler

1.2 kg (6 cups) chopped watermelon
6 kiwifruit, peeled
ice cubes, to serve

Juice the watermelon and kiwifruit through a juice extractor. Stir to
combine and serve over ice. Makes 2 medium glasses.

This drink fixes you up all squeaky-clean on the inside; shame it's not a toner too.

watermelon and guava cleanser

800 g (4 cups) chopped watermelon
3 cm (1¼ inch) piece ginger
7 g (⅓ cup) mint leaves
500 ml (2 cups) guava juice
ice cubes, to serve

Juice the watermelon, ginger and mint through a juice extractor. Stir through the guava juice and serve over ice. Makes 2 large glasses.

watermelon breakfast juice

The ultimate thirst-quencher, watermelon makes a satisfying base for this piquant cooler.

watermelon, grape and peach juice

800 g (4 cups) chopped watermelon
500 g (1 lb 2 oz) green or red seedless grapes
4 peaches, stones removed
2 large passionfruit

Juice the watermelon, grapes and peaches through a juice extractor. Stir through the passionfruit pulp. Makes 2 large glasses.

Been living on the wild side? Give your kidneys a chance to regroup with this healing drink.

kidney cleanser

800 g (4 cups) chopped watermelon
1 large cucumber
3 apples, stalks removed
250 ml (1 cup) cranberry juice

Juice the watermelon, cucumber and apples through a juice extractor. Stir through the cranberry juice. Makes 2 large glasses.

Think plump and juicy when choosing strawberries. Repeat out loud: plump and juicy.

watermelon and strawberry slushy

2 kg (10 cups) chopped watermelon (about 1 large watermelon)
250 g (9 oz) strawberries, hulled
2 teaspoons caster (superfine) sugar

Combine the watermelon, strawberries and sugar in a bowl. Save some watermelon for garnishing. Blend the mixture in batches in a blender until smooth, then pour into a shallow metal tray. Cover with plastic wrap and freeze for 2–3 hours, or until the mixture begins to freeze. Return to the blender and blend quickly to break up the ice. Pour into 6 glasses, then cut the reserved watermelon into 6 small triangles and fix one onto the edge of each glass. Makes 6 medium glasses.

Create a thousand-and-one Arabian Nights of your own with this petal-scented sparkler.

watermelon rosewater slushy

600 g (3 cups) chopped watermelon
1 teaspoon rosewater
1 teaspoon lemon juice
500 ml (2 cups) lemonade

Blend the watermelon in a blender until smooth. Combine with the rosewater, lemon juice and lemonade, then pour into a shallow metal tray. Cover with plastic wrap and freeze for 2 hours, or until just solid around the edges. Return to the blender and blend until thick and slushy. Makes 4 large glasses.

Note: Watermelons are now available almost all year, but tend to be sweeter in the warmer months. Choose one that feels heavy for its size.

watermelon and strawberry slushy

citrus burst Short, sharp, tart, tangy, testy, zesty, mouth-puckering, muscle-clenching, jaw-clinching, eye-popping, shackle-shaking, thirst-quenching, stomach-clutching, sobriety-inducing, temper-tampering, sour-pussing, grizzly-gripping, gusto-making, constitution-shaking, mood-meddling, spine-tingling, total body-cleansing, fleet-of-footing, exhilarating, illuminating and straight-talking citrus! Believe it or not.

The largest of the citrus, grapefruit also pack a punch. Choose heavy fruit with unblemished skins. Pink and ruby varieties are sweeter and result in prettily-coloured juices. Grapefruit can be used in a juicer, with or without the peel (you get more pectin and antioxidants if the peel is added), in the blender, or halved and squeezed on a citrus press. A word of caution: if taking medication, consult your doctor before drinking large doses. The indispensable lemon has a dual purpose in juices. First, for flavour, and second, as a means of preventing fruit such as apples and pears from discolouring. Thin-skinned organic lemons can be juiced without peeling. Otherwise, peel thinly, leaving as much of the white pith as possible, then juice. As with lemons, limes can be used to prevent discolouration of fruits. The flavour also cuts through the richness of other fruits, particularly tropical ones. Roll limes on the bench top to get the most juice out of them. Use on a citrus press or peel and add to a juicer. Buy oranges that feel heavy and have tight skin. Use on a citrus press, juice or blend. Navel oranges are nearly always seedless, so are a good choice. Blood oranges are sweeter and smaller than standard oranges and ensure a great colour in drinks — grab them when in season. Mandarins (and other small citrus such as clementines and tangerines) are smaller and often a bit sweeter than oranges. Juicy clementines have a slight hint of acidity. They go well with warming flavours such as cinnamon and cloves in infused drinks.

Sweet yet light, this is the perfect juice for a more-than-usually delicate morning.

grapefruit, pear and guava

2 grapefruit, peeled
4 pears, stalks removed
375 ml (1½ cups) guava juice
ice cubes, to serve

Juice the grapefruit and pears through a juice extractor. Stir through the guava juice and serve over ice. Makes 2 large glasses.

Pretty in pink with an acid twist — there's nothing sugary about this tart cooler.

pink grapefruit, mint and cranberry juice

2 pink grapefruit
500 ml (2 cups) cranberry juice
2 tablespoons finely chopped mint leaves
ice cubes, to serve

Squeeze the juice from the grapefruit. Stir through the cranberry juice and mint and serve over ice. Makes 2 large glasses.

Drink this baby and you will soon be back in the pink.

think pink

3 pink grapefruit, peeled
250 g (9 oz) strawberries, hulled
375 ml (1 1/2 cups) guava juice
ice cubes, to serve

Juice the grapefruit and strawberries through a juice extractor. Stir through the guava juice and serve over ice. Makes 2 large glasses.

A frou frou fancy for a girly afternoon.

pink pom pom

4 pink grapefruit, peeled
500 g (1 lb 2 oz) black seedless grapes
3 large passionfruit
1 teaspoon pomegranate syrup
honey, to taste
ice cubes, to serve

Juice the grapefruit and grapes through a juice extractor. Stir through the passionfruit pulp, pomegranate syrup and honey and serve over ice. Makes 2 large glasses.

think pink

A delightful mix of tart and fizzy, serve in tulip champagne glasses as a light dessert.

ruby grapefruit and lemon sorbet fizz

500 ml (2 cups) ruby grapefruit juice
250 ml (1 cup) soda water
1 tablespoon caster (superfine) sugar
4 scoops lemon sorbet

Combine the grapefruit juice, soda water and sugar in a jug and chill. Pour into 4 champagne or other glasses and top each with a scoop of sorbet. Makes 4 small glasses.

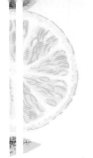

For a nightlife moment without the morning-after hangover,

kick back with a sober mule.

sober mule

3 grapefruit, peeled
7 g (1/3 cup) mint leaves
375 ml (11/2 cups) ginger beer
ice cubes, to serve
2 small mint sprigs, to garnish

Juice the grapefruit and mint through a juice extractor. Stir through the ginger beer and serve over ice, garnished with small mint sprigs. Makes 2 large glasses.

Sometimes all you need is a big hug. If that's not available, this drink is the next best thing.

lemon soother

1/2 lemon, thinly sliced
1 large lemon thyme sprig
1 stem lemon grass, bruised
honey, to taste, optional

Put the lemon, lemon thyme and lemon grass in the base of a large heatproof jug and pour in 1 litre (4 cups) boiling water. Set aside to infuse for 10–15 minutes. Serve hot or warm with some honey, if desired. Makes 4 medium glasses.

This refreshing, slightly tart drink is perfect for a picnic. Just blend with ice, fill a thermos and enjoy the great outdoors.

lemon and green apple thirst quencher

80 ml (1/3 cup) lemon juice
6 green apples, stalks removed
mint leaves, to garnish

Pour the lemon juice into a serving jug. Juice the apples through a juice extractor. Add the apple juice to the lemon juice and stir to combine. Serve garnished with mint leaves. Makes 2 medium glasses.

lemon soother

Beat granny at her own game with this zesty lemon refresher — just make sure you save her a glass.

just-like-grandma-made lemonade

15 lemons
330 g (1 1/2 cups) sugar
ice cubes, to serve
lemon balm leaves, to serve
lemon slices, to serve

Juice the lemons in a citrus press. Put the lemon juice and any pulp in a large non-metallic bowl. Add the sugar and 125 ml (1/2 cup) boiling water and stir until the sugar has dissolved. Add 1.5 litres (6 cups) water and stir well. Transfer to a large jug, add ice cubes and float the lemon balm leaves and lemon slices on top. Makes 6 small glasses.

Running low on funds? Take a tip from childhood and set up a stall of your own.

homemade lemonade

685 ml (2¾ cups) lemon juice
275 g (1¼ cups) caster (superfine) sugar
ice cubes, to serve
mint leaves, to garnish

Combine the lemon juice and sugar in a large bowl and stir until the sugar has dissolved. Pour into a large jug. Add 1.25 litres (5 cups) water, stir well and chill. Serve over ice, garnished with a few mint leaves. Makes 6 medium glasses.

Nutritious and soothing for the stomach, homemade lemon barley water is the real thing.

lemon barley water

110 g (1/2 cup) pearl barley
3 lemons
115 g (1/2 cup) caster (superfine) sugar
crushed ice, to serve
lemon slices, to garnish

Wash the barley well and put in a medium pan. Using a sharp vegetable peeler, remove the zest from the lemons, avoiding the bitter white pith. Juice the lemons in a citrus press. Add the lemon zest and 1.75 litres (7 cups) water to the barley and bring to the boil. Simmer for 30 minutes. Add the sugar and mix well to dissolve. Remove from the heat and set aside to cool. Strain the liquid into a jug and add the lemon juice. Serve over crushed ice, garnished with lemon slices. Makes 4 small glasses.

This sparkling little number will put a spring in your step.

lemon, lime and soda with citrus ice cubes

1 lemon
1 lime
2 1/2 tablespoons lemon juice
170 ml (2/3 cup) lime juice cordial
625 ml (2 1/2 cups) soda water

Using a sharp knife, remove the zest and white pith from the lemon and lime. Cut between the membranes to release the segments. Put a lemon and lime segment in each hole of an ice-cube tray and cover with water. Freeze for 2–3 hours, or until firm. Combine the lemon juice, lime juice cordial and soda water. Pour into 2 glasses and add the ice cubes. Makes 2 medium glasses.

homemade lemonade

Turn up the heat!

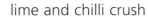

lime and chilli crush

6 limes, peeled
20 g (1 cup) mint leaves
2 teaspoons caster (superfine) sugar
125 ml (1/2 cup) chilled water
ice cubes, to serve
1 chilli, halved lengthways and seeded

Juice the limes and mint through a juice extractor. Stir through the sugar and 125 ml (1/2 cup) water until the sugar has dissolved. Fill 2 medium glasses with ice and place half a chilli in each. Pour in the juice and stir, pressing the chilli gently with the back of a spoon to release some heat. Makes 2 medium glasses.

Get to know this kiwi sparkler and it could be the beginning of a beautiful friendship.

lime and kiwi sparkler

2 limes, peeled
9 kiwifruit, peeled
375 ml (1 1/2 cups) dry ginger ale
mint sprigs, to garnish
lime slices, to garnish
ice cubes, to serve

Juice the limes and kiwifruit through a juice extractor. Stir through the dry ginger ale and serve over ice with a mint sprig and lime slices. Makes 2 large glasses.

Burst onto the scene with this feel-good golden blast.

pine lime and strawberry burst

1 pineapple, peeled
2 limes, peeled
500 g (1 lb 2 oz) strawberries, hulled

Juice the pineapple, limes and strawberries through a juice extractor. Stir to combine. Makes 2 medium glasses.

Take the sting out of an early start with this citrus antidote.

citrus sting

2 limes
3 grapefruit
6 oranges
honey, to taste

Juice the limes, grapefruit and oranges in a citrus press. Stir through the honey. Makes 4 large glasses.

pine lime and strawberry burst

Serve this divine juice with a frangipani flower peeking coyly
over the edge.

orange tropical blossom

4 oranges
1 mango, chopped
1/2 small papaya, peeled, seeded and chopped
1 1/2 teaspoons orange flower water
ice cubes, to serve

Juice the oranges in a citrus press. Blend the orange juice, mango, papaya
and orange flower water in a blender until smooth. Serve over ice. Makes
2 medium glasses.

Playing the field can be fun, but so can sitting on the sidelines — especially with a glass of this in your hand.

green and gold

250 g (9 oz) green seedless grapes
6 oranges, peeled
2 lemons, peeled
1 teaspoon honey

Juice the grapes, oranges and lemons through a juice extractor. Stir through the honey. Makes 2 large glasses.

An extravaganza of succulent stone fruit, tempered with the refreshing tang of oranges.

summer orange

3 oranges, peeled
5 small plums, stones removed
4 peaches, stones removed
10 apricots, stones removed

Juice the oranges, plums, peaches and apricots through a juice extractor. Stir to combine. Makes 2 large glasses.

If only all of our crushes could be so sweet.

orange citrus crush

12 navel oranges
zest and juice of 1 lime
sugar, to taste
ice cubes, to serve

Segment 2 of the oranges and juice the remainder in a citrus press —
don't strain the juice, you can keep the pulp in it. Add the lime zest and
juice to the orange juice. Add the orange segments and sugar. Stir to
combine and serve over ice. Makes 4 medium glasses.

Note: The juice of navel oranges will turn bitter within minutes of juicing,
so drink this juice immediately. Use blood oranges when they're in season.

orange citrus crush

Too old for an ice cream spider? Go for this grown-up version.

orange sorbet soda

500 ml (2 cups) orange juice
250 ml (1 cup) lemonade
2–4 scoops lemon sorbet

Combine the orange juice and lemonade in a jug. Pour into 2 large glasses and top each with 1–2 scoops sorbet. Makes 2 large glasses.

All the colours of the fruity rainbow swirled together.

orange and mixed fruit frappé

10 dried apricot halves
200 g (7 oz) raspberries
1 banana, chopped
1 mango, chopped
500 ml (2 cups) orange juice
1 tablespoon mint leaves
6 ice cubes

Put the dried apricots in a heatproof bowl with 60 ml (¼ cup) boiling water. Set aside for 10 minutes, or until plump, then drain and roughly chop. Blend the apricots, raspberries, banana, mango, orange juice, mint leaves and ice cubes in a blender until smooth. Makes 4 medium glasses.

Transport yourself to Sicily, the home of the best blood oranges, with this deeply flavoursome juice.

blood orange fruit burst

10 apricots, stones removed
250 g (9 oz) strawberries, hulled
250 g (9 oz) lychees, peeled and seeded
375 ml (1½ cups) blood orange juice
ice cubes, to serve

Juice the apricots, strawberries and lychees through a juice extractor. Stir through the blood orange juice and serve over ice. Makes 2 large glasses.

Vamp it up with ruby red blood oranges.

blood orange, fennel and cranberry juice

1 baby fennel
375 ml (1¹/2 cups) blood orange juice
375 ml (1¹/2 cups) cranberry juice
ice cubes, to serve

Juice the baby fennel through a juice extractor. Stir through the blood orange juice and cranberry juice and serve over ice. Makes 2 large glasses.

orange sorbet soda

Suck it in and prepare for the sour cherry punch.

sweet-tart

250 ml (1 cup) blood orange juice
125 ml (½ cup) sour cherry juice
1 tablespoon lime juice
250 ml (1 cup) soda water
ice cubes, to serve

Combine the blood orange juice, sour cherry juice and lime juice in a jug.
Stir through the soda water and serve over ice. Makes 2 large glasses.

The name says it all.

oh my darlin'

3 clementines or small mandarins
5 cm (2 inch) piece ginger, very thinly sliced
2 cinnamon sticks
small pinch ground cloves
1½ tablespoons soft brown sugar

Slice the clementines into rounds and put in a large jug. Add the ginger, cinnamon, cloves, brown sugar and 1 litre (4 cups) boiling water. Stir to combine, pressing against the clementines to help release the juice and flavour. Set aside to infuse for about 10 minutes before serving warm. Makes 4 medium glasses.

You won't know what hit you.

mandarin and passionfruit shots

6 mandarins, peeled
1 panama or large passionfruit

Juice the mandarins through a juice extractor. Strain the passionfruit pulp and discard the seeds, reserving a few for garnish if desired. Stir the passionfruit juice through the mandarin juice and chill well. Stir to combine and serve garnished with the reserved passionfruit seeds, if desired. Makes 4 shot glasses.

Just the thing after a tiring afternoon on the croquet lawn.

mandarin rose

375 ml (1½ cups) mandarin juice
1 teaspoon rosewater
2 teaspoons pomegranate syrup
250 ml (1 cup) soda water or lemonade
ice cubes, to serve

Combine the mandarin juice, rosewater, pomegranate syrup and soda water or lemonade in a jug. Serve over ice. Makes 2 large glasses.

mandarin and passionfruit shots

the vegetable garden Just like getting sand between the toes, this chapter is all about getting soil between the teeth. No matter how much you scrub some of these fellas, you'll never convince them to shed their earthy goodness. As someone once said, you can take the carrot out of the garden but you can't take the garden out of the carrot. The uninitiated may like to start with small servings of these healthy elixirs.

Super rich in iron and beta-carotenes, beetroot is not for the mild-mannered juicer. Cut its earthy richness with citrus. To prepare, give beetroot a seriously good scrubbing and cut off any green stems. Cut the crown away, chop and add to the juicer. Sweet carrots make a great base juice and are limited only by the fact that they oxidize quickly. Use with citrus juice to help prevent this. Trim tops, then juice. Salty, watery celery needs rinsing under running water before juicing; add the leaves too, if you want. Buy celery with crisp, fresh stems. For sheer refreshing good value, try cucumber. Choose firm ones (the variety doesn't really matter) with no signs of bruising and store in the refrigerator, wrapped in plastic. No need to peel, just wash and juice. fennel is a funny one. Just when you think you've discovered every way that it can be prepared, along comes another, such as juicing. Use baby bulbs where possible, or larger, more mature ones for a headier flavour. garlic embodies the great and good from the garden. Peel the cloves before you juice. green leafy vegetables like spinach and watercress are excellent sources of antioxidants and phytochemicals. Use leaves straight from the refrigerator, while they are still a bit stiff, or juice with other ingredients. Rinse spinach well or soak in ice-cold water for 1–2 minutes to get rid of sand and grit. Leaves and herbs need to be bundled together or alternated with other, juicier ingredients. Juice on slow. Use good quality tomatoes to get the best flavour and nutritional value.

213

Add body and bounce to your natural vitality with this spicy little number.

vitalizing beetroot, carrot and ginger juice

1 beetroot, scrubbed
6 carrots
3 cm (1¼ inch) piece ginger, peeled

Juice the beetroot, carrots and ginger through a juice extractor. Stir to combine. Makes 2 small glasses.

Down a tumbler of this nourishing blend for a de-tox that matches style with substance.

dinner in a glass

1 beetroot, scrubbed
10–12 carrots
2 green apples, stalks removed
2 English spinach leaves
2 celery stalks

Juice the beetroot, carrots, apples, spinach and celery through a juice extractor. Stir to combine and serve chilled. Makes 2 large glasses.

There's no better way to beet it!

beetroot, rockmelon, ginger and mint juice

500 g (1 lb 2 oz) beetroot, scrubbed
¼ medium-sized rockmelon (or other orange-fleshed melon),
  peeled, seeded and chopped
2 tablespoons roughly chopped ginger
2 tablespoons mint leaves

Juice the beetroot, rockmelon, ginger and mint through a juice extractor.
Stir to combine. Makes 4 medium glasses.

Too good for you? There's simply no such thing.

too good for you

6 carrots
1 large apple, cored
4 celery stalks, including leaves
6 iceberg lettuce leaves
20 English spinach leaves
ice cubes, to serve

Juice the carrots, apple, celery, lettuce and spinach through a juice extractor. Stir to combine and serve over ice. Makes 4 small glasses.

vitalizing beetroot, carrot and ginger juice

I can see clearly now my juicer's here.

220

honeyed carrots

1 kg (2 lb 4 oz) carrots
125 g (4½ oz) alfalfa sprouts
4 pears, stalks removed
1–2 teaspoons honey, to taste

Juice the carrots, alfalfa and pears through a juice extractor. Stir through the honey. Garnish with carrot strips, if desired. Makes 2 medium glasses.

Without a doubt, baby carrots are the sweetest of the bunch.

carrot, apricot and nectarine

1 kg (2 lb 4 oz) baby carrots
10 apricots, stones removed
4 large nectarines, stones removed
ice cubes, to serve
lemon slices, to serve

Juice the carrots, apricots and nectarines through a juice extractor. Stir to combine and serve over ice with lemon slices. Makes 2 large glasses.

When the body isn't the temple it should be, give it a boost with iron-rich tomato.

222   carrot, tomato, lemon and basil juice

1 kg (2 lb 4 oz) carrots
4 vine-ripened tomatoes
1 lemon, peeled
10 g (1/3 cup) basil leaves

Juice the carrots, tomatoes, lemon and basil through a juice extractor. Stir to combine. Makes 2 medium glasses.

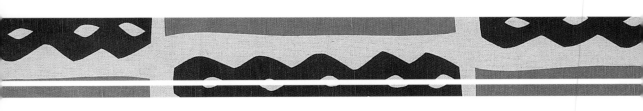

After one cocktail too many, the road to recovery is definitely paved orange.

carrot cocktail

10–12 carrots
125 ml (1/2 cup) pineapple juice
125 ml (1/2 cup) orange juice
1–2 teaspoons honey, to taste
8 ice cubes

Juice the carrots through a juice extractor. Stir through the pineapple juice, orange juice, honey and ice cubes. Makes 2 medium glasses.

honeyed carrots

Cleanse your palate and freshen your breath with a serious hit of parsley.

celery, parsley and tomato juice

20 g (1 cup) parsley
6 vine-ripened tomatoes
4 celery stalks
celery stalks, extra, to garnish

Juice the parsley, tomatoes and celery through a juice extractor. Chill well, then stir to combine. Serve garnished with a celery stalk swizzle stick. Makes 2 large glasses.

Note: For extra spice, add a few drops of Tabasco sauce and freshly ground black pepper.

Be a killer queen with this potent concoction and shoot down those germs in style.

cold killer

4 celery stalks
1 kg (2 lb 4 oz) carrots
2 garlic cloves
10 g (1/2 cup) flat-leaf (Italian) parsley
2 teaspoons honey

Juice the celery, carrots, garlic and parsley through a juice extractor. Stir through the honey. Makes 2 medium glasses.

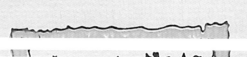

Even the meanest machine needs the occasional tune-up.

green machine

6 celery stalks
2 apples, stalks removed
125 g (4¹/2 oz) alfalfa sprouts
10 g (¹/2 cup) flat-leaf (Italian) parsley
10 g (¹/2 cup) mint leaves

Juice the celery, apples, alfalfa, parsley and mint through a juice extractor.
Stir to combine. Makes 2 medium glasses.

Sticks and stones may break my bones but juice helps me forget all about it.

sticks and stones

6 celery stalks
5 small peaches, stones removed
1/2 lemon, peeled
7 g (1/4 cup) basil leaves
ice cubes, to serve

Juice the celery, peaches, lemon and basil through a juice extractor. Stir to combine and serve over ice. Makes 2 medium glasses.

green machine

Don't be a dill, revive and survive with this smart concoction.

cucumber, apple and dill juice

2 large cucumbers
9 apples, stalks removed
2 tablespoons dill
1 lemon, peeled
ice cubes, to serve

Juice the cucumbers, apples, dill and lemon through a juice extractor. Stir
to combine and serve over ice. Makes 2 medium glasses.

Enhance your cool factor with a chilled shot of cucumber.

cool as a cucumber

3 large cucumbers
3 limes, peeled
20 g (1 cup) mint leaves
1 1/2 tablespoons caster (superfine) sugar

Juice the cucumbers, limes and mint through a juice extractor. Stir through
the sugar. Makes 2 large glasses.

Beet yourself up at the end of winter and get yourself into the mood for spring.

spring clean

2 large cucumbers, peeled
6 carrots
1 large green apple, stalk removed
2 celery stalks, including leaves
1 large beetroot, scrubbed
ice cubes, to serve

Juice the cucumbers, carrots, apple, celery and beetroot through a juice extractor. Stir to combine and serve over ice. Makes 4 small glasses.

Calm the troubled waters of your tummy with this gentle soothing tonic.

savoury soother

1 kg (2 lb 4 oz) cucumbers
1 lime, peeled
10 g (¹/₃ cup) coriander (cilantro) leaves
1 garlic clove
1 small avocado, peeled, stone removed
large pinch ground cumin

Juice the cucumbers, lime, coriander and garlic through a juice extractor. Transfer to a blender with the avocado and cumin and blend until smooth. Makes 2 small glasses.

cool as a cucumber

Tender young fennel bulbs add a fresh, astringent liquorice kick to good old apple and orange juice.

fennel, apple and orange juice

1 baby fennel, outer leaves removed
3 apples, stalks removed
6 oranges, peeled
7 g (1/4 cup) basil leaves
1 teaspoon honey, optional

Juice the fennel, apples, oranges and basil through a juice extractor. Stir through the honey, if desired. Makes 2 large glasses.

For a liquorice sting, choose a larger bulb of fennel.

fennel and orange juice

8 oranges
150 g (5¹/2 oz) baby fennel, outer leaves removed

Peel and quarter the oranges. Juice the fennel through a juice extractor to release the flavours, then juice the orange and chill well. Stir to combine. Makes 2 medium glasses.

Note: When in season, larger, more developed fennel will have a stronger flavour than baby fennel.

Your mum always told you to eat your greens, but better still, drink them!

green shot

30 g (1½ cups) flat-leaf (Italian) parsley
1 medium cucumber
½ teaspoon caster (superfine) sugar
½ teaspoon lemon juice

Juice the parsley and cucumber through a juice extractor, saving a little cucumber for garnishing. Stir through the sugar until the sugar has fully dissolved. Chill well, then stir through the lemon juice and garnish with cucumber sticks. Serve immediately. Makes 6 shot glasses.

One, two, three … down the hatch.

herbal tonic

20 g (1 cup) flat-leaf (Italian) parsley
20 g (1 cup) mint leaves
15 g (1/2 cup) coriander (cilantro) leaves
3 cm (1 1/4 inch) piece ginger
500 ml (2 cups) tonic water
ice cubes, to serve

Juice the parsley, mint, coriander and ginger through a juice extractor then add 2 tablespoons water to help push the juice through. Stir through the tonic water and serve over ice. Makes 2 large glasses.

green shot

Why didn't we know of this blend when we were really hitting our straps? Prepare and drink just before heading out.

basil, spearmint and liquorice wake-me-up

1 tablespoon liquorice tea leaves
1 tablespoon spearmint tea leaves
10 basil leaves
basil leaves, extra, to serve

Put the liquorice and spearmint tea leaves into a teapot. Lightly crush the basil leaves and add them to the pot. Fill the pot with boiling water (about 1 litre/4 cups), put on the lid and leave to brew for 3 minutes. Strain into teacups and garnish with basil leaves. Serve hot or cold. Makes 2 glasses.

Note: As the tea cools, the liquorice flavour becomes stronger and sweeter — add a few slices of lemon if you find it too strong.

Mint juleps are just the ticket when the in-laws visit, but try to stay off the bourbon.

mint julep

20 g (1 cup) mint leaves, roughly chopped
1 tablespoon sugar
1 tablespoon lemon juice
250 ml (1 cup) pineapple juice
250 ml (1 cup) dry ginger ale
ice cubes, to serve
mint leaves, to garnish

Roughly chop the mint leaves and put in a heatproof jug with the sugar. Using a wooden spoon, bruise the mint. Add the lemon juice, pineapple juice and 125 ml (1/2 cup) boiling water, and mix well. Cover with plastic wrap and set aside for 30 minutes. Strain, then chill. Just before serving, stir through the dry ginger ale and serve over ice, garnished with mint leaves. Makes 2 medium glasses.

Sweet memories in a glass.

rosemary and apple infusion

12 apples, juiced and strained or 1 litre (4 cups) bottled apple
  juice
1 rosemary sprig
55 g (1/4 cup) caster (superfine) sugar

Combine the apple juice, rosemary and sugar in a large saucepan over high heat and stir until the sugar has dissolved. Bring to the boil, then remove from the heat. Allow to infuse for at least 1 minute, depending on your preferred strength of rosemary flavour. Strain and serve either warm or well chilled. Makes 4 medium glasses.

Are you going to Scarborough Fair?

sage, rosemary, celery and carrot juice

2¹/₂ tablespoons sage leaves
2¹/₂ tablespoons rosemary leaves
8 celery stalks
3 carrots
ice cubes, to serve

Juice the sage, rosemary, celery and carrots through a juice extractor in that order so that the vegetables help to push the herb juice through. Stir to combine and serve over ice. Makes 2 medium glasses.

basil, spearmint and liquorice wake-me-up

Life can be a marathon *and* a sprint, so when you need a fuel injection, reach for the juicer.

spinach energizer

50 g (2 cups) baby English spinach leaves
1 large cucumber
3 apples, stalks removed
3 celery stalks
1 baby fennel
10 g (1/2 cup) parsley

Juice the spinach, cucumber, apples, celery, fennel and parsley through a juice extractor. Stir to combine. Makes 2 large glasses.

Butterflies can flutter at any time. Soothe them away with this calming tonic.

tummy calmer

50 g (2 cups) English spinach leaves
400 g (14 oz) cabbage
4 apples, stalks removed

Juice the spinach, cabbage and apples through a juice extractor. Stir to combine. Makes 2 small glasses.

Prepare for blast-off.

rocket fuel

150 g (5$\frac{1}{2}$ oz) rocket (arugula)
10 g ($\frac{1}{2}$ cup) mint leaves
1 cm ($\frac{1}{2}$ inch) piece ginger
$\frac{1}{2}$ garlic clove
pinch ground cumin
300 ml (10$\frac{1}{2}$ fl oz) apple juice

Juice the rocket, mint, ginger and garlic through a juice extractor then add
1 tablespoon water to help push the juice through. Stir through the cumin
and apple juice. Makes 4 shot glasses.

How's this for a good intestinal cleanser?

waterworks

30 g (1 cup) watercress leaves
4 celery stalks
1 spring onion (scallion), chopped
1¹/₂ cucumbers
ice cubes, to serve

Juice the watercress, celery, spring onion and cucumber through a juice extractor. Stir to combine and serve over ice. Makes 2 medium glasses.

spinach energizer

Knocks a virgin mary into touch — spicy, hot and red in tooth and claw.

gazpacho in a glass

6 vine-ripened tomatoes
1 red capsicum (pepper)
1 lemon, peeled
2 large cucumbers
10 g (1/2 cup) parsley
1 garlic clove
dash Tabasco sauce
ice cubes, to serve
extra virgin olive oil, to serve, optional

Juice the tomatoes, capsicum, lemon, cucumbers, parsley and garlic through a juice extractor. Stir through the Tabasco, to taste. Serve over ice with a drizzle of extra virgin olive oil, if desired. Makes 2 large glasses.

This drink is a seriously good tipple in its own right, but if you must add a slug of vodka, we promise not to tell.

virgin mary

750 ml (3 cups) tomato juice
1 tablespoon Worcestershire sauce
2 tablespoons lemon juice
1/4 teaspoon ground nutmeg
few drops Tabasco sauce
12 ice cubes
2 lemon slices, halved

Put the tomato juice, Worcestershire sauce, lemon juice, nutmeg and Tabasco sauce in a large jug and stir to combine. Blend the ice cubes in a blender for 30 seconds, or until the ice is crushed to 125 ml (1/2 cup). Pour the tomato juice mixture into 4 glasses and add the crushed ice and lemon slices. Season with salt and pepper. Makes 4 small glasses.

For those days when you just can't make up your mind.

sweet and sour

4 vine-ripened tomatoes
3 oranges, peeled
10 g (1/2 cup) mint leaves
1 teaspoon caster (superfine) sugar
1 teaspoon balsamic vinegar
ice cubes, to serve

Juice the tomatoes, oranges and mint leaves through a juice extractor. Stir through the sugar and balsamic vinegar until the sugar has dissolved. Serve over ice. Makes 2 medium glasses.

This is no ordinary tomato juice. It's much bigger than that.

big red

250 ml (1 cup) tomato juice
250 ml (1 cup) apricot nectar
large pinch ground ginger
pinch ground cardamom
small pinch ground cloves
ice cubes, to serve

Combine the tomato juice, apricot nectar, ginger, cardamom and cloves in a large jug, then chill well. Stir to combine and serve over ice. Makes 2 large glasses.

gazpacho in a glass

cinnamon, spice and all things nice The spice cupboard is a many splendoured thing: cloves and vanilla beans, cardamom pods, cinnamon sticks and aromatic nutmeg. Pound or grind, pulp and chop,

blend and infuse your way to soothing brews. Not every juice has to be all snap and crackle, you know. Look deep into your cupboard and discover ingredients full of depth and character, just waiting their turn.

Luxuriously aromatic, flower waters such as orange and rose are needed in small amounts only. Follow recipe suggestions. Fresh flowers such as lavender and edible rose petals are useful too: infuse and strain. Good old ginger. Knobbly, beige-coloured and a rhizome to boot, but still we can't get enough of it. With good reason, too: it calms an upset tummy, aids the digestion and gets a sluggish circulation into action. Generally, no need to peel or slice, just wash and use in the juicer. If it's fibrous, it may be easier to grate. Ground spices such as cardamom, cinnamon, cloves and cumin are great for adding warmth and depth to drinks. In their whole form, cardamom pods and cinnamon sticks can be used in infused drinks; freshly grated nutmeg brings a spicy warmth; and star anise adds a mild liquorice edge to drinks. For the best flavour, use the fresh spice if possible and grind it yourself as needed. A sticky, sweet-sour pulp, tamarind is sold in blocks that contain the plant's seeds or as ready-made concentrated paste in jars. To use, cut off a little, mix with hot water, then press through a sieve with a spoon to extract the pulp. Store in the refrigerator for up to a year. The humble tea bag isn't so humble after all. In infusions they go particularly well with citrus and fresh herbs. Good-quality vanilla pods have a warm, caramel vanilla aroma and flavour, and should be soft, not hard or dry. You can also use natural vanilla extract (essence) but beware of cheap copies. The pod can be reused: wash in cold water, then dry and store.

Use honey and vanilla to coax out the natural sweetness of the humble carrot.

cardamom, carrot and orange juice

1 kg (2 lb 4 oz) carrots
6 oranges, peeled
small pinch ground cardamom
1 teaspoon natural vanilla extract (essence)
1 teaspoon honey
ice cubes, to serve

Juice the carrots and oranges through a juice extractor. Stir through the cardamom, vanilla and honey, and serve over ice. Makes 2 large glasses.

Subtly spiced, this refreshing tea is a perfect match for a light lunch and salad.

cardamom and orange tea

3 cardamom pods
250 ml (1 cup) orange juice
3 strips orange zest
2 tablespoons caster (superfine) sugar
ice cubes, to serve

Put the cardamom pods on a chopping board and crack them open by pressing with the side of a large knife. Put the cardamom, orange juice, orange zest, sugar and 500 ml (2 cups) water into a pan. Stir over medium heat for 10 minutes, or until the sugar has dissolved. Bring to the boil, then remove from the heat. Set aside to infuse for 2–3 hours, or until cold, then chill. Strain and serve over ice. Makes 2 medium glasses.

Use the best quality maple syrup you can find, then make this for your favourite mountie.

cinnamon, maple and pear frappé

400 g (14 oz) canned pears in natural juice
1/2 teaspoon ground cinnamon
1 1/2 tablespoons pure maple syrup
12 large ice cubes

Blend the pears and juice, maple syrup, cinnamon and ice cubes in a blender until smooth. Makes 2 large glasses.

Steeping the fruit and spices deepens the flavour of this golden infusion

cinnamon and apple tea infusion

1 cinnamon stick
4 golden delicious apples, roughly chopped
3–4 tablespoons soft brown sugar
ice cubes, to serve

Put the cinnamon stick, apple, brown sugar and 1 litre (4 cups) water into a pan. Bring to the boil, then reduce the heat and gently simmer for 10–15 minutes, or until the flavours have infused and the apple has softened. Remove from the heat and cool slightly, then chill. Strain and serve over lots of ice. Makes 2 medium glasses.

cinnamon, maple and pear frappé

Carrot and lime receive a fragrant lift through the addition of rosewater and cinnamon in this Arabian-Nights-inspired drink.

rosewater, carrot and lime juice

1.5 kg (3 lb 5 oz) carrots
3 limes, peeled
1 teaspoon rosewater
large pinch ground cinnamon
ice cubes, to serve

Juice the carrots and limes through a juice extractor. Stir through the rosewater and cinnamon and serve over ice. Makes 2 medium glasses.

Sweet and exotic, this juice is perfect for a languid late afternoon tea.

turkish delight

2–3 lemons, to taste
1 teaspoon rosewater
2 teaspoons honey
ice cubes, to serve

Juice the lemons in a citrus press. Stir through the rosewater, honey and 375 ml (1¹/₂ cups) cold water. Serve over ice. Makes 2 large glasses.

Play it again, Sam. Evoke the romance of Casablanca with this fragrant and exotic juice.

orange blossom citrus refresher

6 oranges, peeled
20 g (1 cup) mint leaves
1½ teaspoons orange flower water
1 teaspoon pomegranate syrup
ice cubes, to serve
mint sprigs, to garnish
pomegranate syrup, extra, to serve, optional

Juice the oranges and mint leaves through a juice extractor. Stir through the orange flower water and pomegranate syrup and serve over ice, garnished with mint. Drizzle over a little more pomegranate syrup, if desired. Makes 2 medium glasses.

Create your own costume drama with this ladylike tonic.

lavender and rose lemonade

juice and zest of 2 lemons
15 g (1/2 oz) English lavender flowers, stripped from their stems
110 g (1 1/2 cups) sugar
1/2 teaspoon rosewater
edible pale pink rose petals, to garnish, optional

Put the lemon zest, lavender flowers, sugar and 500 ml (2 cups) boiling water into a heatproof jug and mix well. Cover with plastic wrap and set aside for 15 minutes. Strain, then stir through the lemon juice, rosewater and enough cold water to make 1 litre (4 cups). Chill well. Stir to combine and serve garnished with rose petals, if desired. Makes 6 small glasses.

Note: Add more water, if preferred, for a milder flavour.

lavender and rose lemonade

Strong and spicy, line up the shot glasses and find out who's really the tough guy.

red ginger

500 g (1 lb 2 oz) red seedless grapes
10 small plums, stones removed
2 limes, peeled
3 cm (1¼ inch) piece ginger
10 g (½ cup) mint leaves
ice cubes, to serve

Juice the grapes, plums, limes, ginger and mint through a juice extractor. Stir to combine and serve over ice. Makes 4 shot glasses.

Just what you need to get yourself into gear when time is short and the to-do list is long.

pineapple ginger kick

1/2 pineapple, peeled
3 oranges, peeled
3.5 cm (1 1/2 inch) piece ginger
ice cubes, to serve

Juice the pineapple, oranges and ginger through a juice extractor. Stir to combine and serve over ice. Makes 2 small glasses.

Recover in style with the ultimate tummy soother.

ginger, lemon and mint soother

2 cm (3/4 inch) piece ginger, thinly sliced
125 ml (1/2 cup) lemon juice
2 1/2 tablespoons honey
1 tablespoon mint leaves
ice cubes, to serve

Put the ginger, lemon juice, honey, mint and 750 ml (3 cups) boiling water into a heatproof jug. Set aside to infuse for 2–3 hours, or until cold. Strain and chill. Stir to combine and serve over ice. Makes 4 small glasses.

Note: This drink is delicious served the next day as all the flavours will have had time to infuse together.

If in need of a little get up and go, get a little of this.

gingered melon juice

1 honeydew melon, peeled, seeded and chopped
1 rockmelon (or other orange-fleshed melon), peeled,
  seeded and chopped
2 cm (3/4 inch) piece ginger

Juice the honeydew, rockmelon and ginger through a juice extractor. Stir
to combine. Makes 2 large glasses.

red ginger

Instant winter warming with a zing of ginger and a healthy dose of vitamins.

warm ginger and carrot shots

2 kg (4 1b 8 oz) carrots
4 cm (1½ inch) piece ginger
1 tablespoon lemon juice
large pinch ground cinnamon
large pinch ground cumin
natural yoghurt, to serve, optional

Juice the carrots and ginger through a juice extractor. Transfer to a saucepan with the lemon juice, cinnamon and cumin. Stir over medium heat until just warmed through then pour into shot glasses or tall glasses. Top each glass with a small dollop of yoghurt and slightly swirl through. Makes 8 shot glasses or 2 large glasses.

Breath deep and inhale the soothing aromas — a dreamy break is on its way.

ginger and lemon calm

3 cm (1¼ inch) piece ginger, sliced
1 lemon, thinly sliced
1 chamomile tea bag
honey, to taste

Put the ginger, lemon and tea bag in the bottom of a plunger or heatproof bowl and pour in 1 litre (4 cups) boiling water. Set aside to infuse for 10 minutes before plunging or straining. Serve with a little honey. Makes 4 small glasses.

Flush away any irritations with this spicy, cleansing tonic.

spiced cranberry infusion

1 litre (4 cups) cranberry juice
80 g (1/3 cup) caster (superfine) sugar
5 cm (2 inch) piece ginger, sliced
3 strips orange zest
2 cinnamon sticks
small pinch ground cloves
orange slices, to garnish, optional

Put the cranberry juice, sugar, ginger, orange zest, cinnamon sticks and cloves into a large saucepan. Stir over high heat until the sugar has dissolved. Bring to the boil, then turn off the heat but leave on the hotplate to infuse for 15 minutes. Strain and serve warm, garnished with a slice of orange, if desired. Makes 4 small glasses.

This is just the ticket to help you through an afternoon slump.

warm ginger zinger

10 cm (4 inch) piece ginger, very thinly sliced
1 teaspoon white peppercorns
1 star anise
1 cinnamon stick
honey, to taste

Put the ginger, peppercorns, star anise and cinnamon in a large heatproof
jug and pour in 1 litre (4 cups) boiling water. Set aside to infuse for about
15 minutes. Serve with honey. Makes 4 medium glasses.

warm ginger and carrot shots

You know it's good for you but you never knew it could taste so damn good.

iced kiwi green tea

6 kiwifruit, peeled
1 lemon, thinly sliced
2 green tea bags
2 tablespoons caster (superfine) sugar
ice cubes, to serve
kiwifruit slices, to serve
lemon slices, to serve

Juice the kiwifruit through a juice extractor. Put the lemon slices, tea bags and 1.25 litres (5 cups) boiling water into a heatproof bowl. Set aside to infuse for 5 minutes. Strain and discard the tea bags. Add the kiwifruit juice and sugar and stir until the sugar has dissolved. Set aside to cool, then chill. Stir to combine and serve over ice, garnished with a slice each of kiwifruit and lemon. Makes 4 medium glasses.

If no one is watching, pop the tea bags over your eyes while you wait for this refreshing brew to chill.

iced lemon and peppermint tea

2 peppermint tea bags
6 thick strips lemon zest
1 tablespoon sugar, or to taste
ice cubes, to serve
mint leaves, to garnish

Put the tea bags, lemon zest and 830 ml (3 1/3 cups) boiling water into a heatproof bowl. Set aside to infuse for 5 minutes. Squeeze out and discard the tea bags. Stir in the sugar and chill. Stir to combine and serve over ice, garnished with mint leaves. Makes 2 medium glasses.

Note: Alternatively, pour about 125 ml (1/2 cup) of the tea mixture into 8 holes of an ice-cube tray. Freeze and serve with the chilled tea.

This herbal hit will have you skipping all the way to work.

iced mint tea

4 peppermint tea bags
115 g (1/3 cup) honey
500 ml (2 cups) grapefruit juice
250 ml (1 cup) orange juice
mint sprigs, to garnish

Put the tea bags and 750 ml (3 cups) boiling water into a large heatproof jug. Set aside to infuse for 3 minutes. Discard the tea bags. Stir through the honey and set aside to cool. Stir through the grapefruit and orange juice, cover and chill. Stir to combine and serve garnished with mint sprigs. Makes 6 small glasses.

Develop a taste for island living with this piquant brew.

minty pineapple iced tea

1 pineapple or 500 ml (2 cups) pineapple juice
2 English breakfast tea bags
10 g (1/2 cup) mint leaves
ice cubes, to serve
mint sprigs, to garnish

Juice the pineapple through a juice extractor, then strain the juice. Put the tea bags, mint leaves and 1.25 litres (5 cups) boiling water into a large heatproof bowl. Set aside to infuse for 5 minutes. Discard the tea bags and mint. Stir through the pineapple juice and chill. Stir to combine and serve over ice, garnished with mint sprigs. Makes 4 medium glasses.

iced kiwi green tea

Sweet yet subtle, this is a brew to daydream over.

iced orange and strawberry tea

3 oranges, peeled
500 g (1 lb 2 oz) strawberries, hulled
2 orange pekoe tea bags
ice cubes, to serve
orange zest, to garnish, optional

Juice the oranges and strawberries through a juice extractor. Put the tea bags and 1.25 litres (5 cups) boiling water in a heatproof bowl. Set aside to infuse for 5 minutes. Discard the tea bags. Stir through the orange and strawberry juice. Chill well. Stir to combine and serve over ice with a twist of orange zest, if desired. Makes 4 medium glasses.

Darjeeling, darling, is the only tea in town.

orange and ginger tea cooler

1 tablespoon Darjeeling tea leaves
zest of 1 small orange, cut into long, thin strips
250 ml (1 cup) ginger beer
8 thin slices glacé ginger
2 tablespoons sugar
4–6 ice cubes
mint leaves, to garnish

Put the tea leaves, half the orange zest and 500 ml (2 cups) boiling water in a heatproof bowl. Cover and set aside to infuse for 5 minutes. Strain through a fine strainer into a jug. Stir through the ginger beer and chill for 6 hours, or preferably overnight. An hour before serving, stir through the glacé ginger, sugar and remaining orange zest. Stir to combine, pour into tall glasses, add 2–3 ice cubes per glass and garnish with mint leaves. Makes 2 medium glasses.

When you fancy an old-fashioned afternoon tea party, sip this on the porch and see who comes a knockin'.

american iced tea

4 Ceylon tea bags
2 tablespoons sugar
2 tablespoons lemon juice
375 ml (1½ cups) dark grape juice
500 ml (2 cups) orange juice
375 ml (1½ cups) dry ginger ale
ice cubes, to serve
lemon slices, to serve

Put the tea bags and 1 litre (4 cups) boiling water in a heatproof bowl. Set aside to infuse for 3 minutes. Discard the tea bags. Stir through the sugar and set aside to cool. Stir through the lemon juice, grape juice and orange juice, and chill. Stir through the dry ginger ale and serve over ice with a slice of lemon. Makes 8 small glasses.

Smoky and seductive, this sophisticated tea makes storm clouds disappear.

earl grey summer tea

250 ml (1 cup) orange juice
2 teaspoons finely grated orange zest
1 tablespoon Earl Grey tea leaves
1 cinnamon stick
2 tablespoons sugar, or to taste
ice cubes, to serve
1 orange, thinly sliced into rounds
4 cinnamon sticks, extra, to garnish

Put the orange juice, orange zest, tea leaves, cinnamon stick and 750 ml (3 cups) water into a medium saucepan. Slowly bring to a simmer over gentle heat. Add the sugar and stir until the sugar has dissolved. Remove from the heat and set aside to cool. Strain the liquid into a jug and chill. Stir to combine and serve with lots of ice cubes, garnished with the orange slices and extra cinnamon sticks. Makes 4 small glasses.

iced orange and strawberry tea

Classy as a cordial, this syrup also makes a divine sorbet.

lime and lemon grass syrup

4 limes
3–4 stems lemon grass, bruised and cut into 10 cm (4 inch) lengths
5 cm (2 inch) piece ginger, chopped
145 g (2/3 cup) caster (superfine) sugar

Juice the limes in a citrus press. Put the lime juice, lemon grass, ginger, sugar and 2 litres (8 cups) water in a large saucepan. Stir over high heat until the sugar has dissolved. Bring to the boil and cook for 1 1/2 hours, or until reduced to about 375 ml (1 1/2 cups). Set aside to cool, then strain. Makes 375 ml (1 1/2 cups).

Note: To serve, pour a little syrup into a glass with ice and top with soda water or lemonade. Use stems of lemon grass as swizzle sticks.

A fragrant tonic for the soul as well as the body.

citrus and lemon grass tea

3 stems lemon grass
2 slices lemon
3 teaspoons honey, or to taste
ice cubes, to serve
lemon slices, extra, to serve

Discard the first two tough outer layers of the lemon grass. Thinly slice the lemon grass and put into a heatproof jug with 625 ml (2 1/2 cups) boiling water. Add the lemon slices, cover and set aside to infuse and cool to room temperature. Strain, stir through the honey, and chill. Stir to combine and serve over ice with lemon slices. Makes 2 medium glasses.

Note: For maximum flavour, only use the bottom third of the lemon grass stems (the white part). Use the trimmed stems as a garnish.

Mouth-puckeringly tart when straight, a dash of sugar makes tamarind lip-smackingly good.

tamarind cooler

2 teaspoons tamarind concentrate
3 tablespoons caster (superfine) sugar
20 g (1 cup) mint leaves
12 large ice cubes

Blend the tamarind, sugar, mint, ice cubes and 250 ml (1 cup) water in a blender until smooth. Makes 2 medium glasses.

A great winter blend, this will soon have you feeling warm and calm all over.

vanilla and apricot orange infusion

200 g (7 oz) dried apricots, chopped
1 vanilla bean, chopped
zest of 1 orange
55 g (¼ cup) caster (superfine) sugar
small pinch cloves, optional
ice cubes, to serve

Combine the apricots, vanilla bean, orange zest, sugar, cloves and 3 litres (12 cups) water in a large saucepan. Stir over high heat until the sugar has dissolved. Bring to the boil, then reduce the heat and gently simmer for 20 minutes. Set aside to cool. Strain and chill well. Stir to combine and serve over ice. Makes 6 medium glasses.

vanilla and apricot orange infusion

creamy concoctions Welcome to the world of the blender. A place of creamy, dreamy, silky, smoothy, cruisy, woozy, bluesy blends. We're talking no more Mr Second Fiddle, no more Mr Waiting in the Wings for the blender — dairy-based drinks are where it's at. Low-fat, no-fat, whole cream milk, even buttermilk: it loves them all. Fruit yoghurts, frozen yoghurts: perfect! Ice cream: delicious!

Weighing in at around 10 percent fat content, ice cream adds
an unbeatable rich and creamy texture to smoothies. The better quality
the ice cream, the better the resulting drink. Home-made ice creams
made with raw eggs should be eaten within 3 days. Those without eggs
will keep for longer but their flavour may change as they age. Be it skim,
semi-skimmed or whole, milk is the bedrock upon which all other
smoothies stand. Packed with calcium, protein and vitamins A and D
(absent, however, from skimmed milks) it combines well with everything
from macadamia nuts to figs. Lower fat milks result in a more watery
drink. Buttermilk is made from pasteurized skim milk to which an acid-
producing bacteria is added, thickening it and giving it a tangy taste. If
using buttermilk in place of whole milk, omit any lemon or lime. Live
yoghurt can support the digestive system by restoring natural
gut bacteria. Of course, it also tastes good. Blend with well-established
winners such as banana, mango and lime, but try also dried apricots,
avocado and prunes. Don't worry overly if the low-fat wild berry yoghurt
required by a recipe isn't available. Choose a similar one; the result will
be just as good. Smoothies are ideal places for healthy additives
to hide. Try sweet-tasting malted milk powder, made from dried and
ground barley grains, or raw wheat germ, the extracted embryo of the
wheat grain. Store wheat germ in the refrigerator, as it will go rancid
due to its high oil content. Buy both from health food stores.

311

Best consumed on a Sunday with the papers by one hand and some waffles by the other.

blue maple

200 g (1 cup) low-fat blueberry fromage frais
185 ml (3/4 cup) low-fat milk
1 tablespoon maple syrup
1/2 teaspoon ground cinnamon
300 g (10 1/2 oz) frozen blueberries

Blend the fromage frais, milk, maple syrup, cinnamon and 250 g (9 oz) of the frozen blueberries in a blender until smooth. Serve topped with the remaining blueberries. Makes 2 medium glasses.

It's creamy, it's cold and it's berry, berry good.

berry slushy

300 g (10½ oz) frozen blueberries
150 g (5½ oz) raspberries
200 g (7 oz) vanilla yoghurt
250 ml (1 cup) milk
1 tablespoon wheat germ

Blend the frozen blueberries in a blender in short burts until starting to
break up. Add the raspberries, yoghurt, milk and wheat germ and blend
until smooth. Makes 2 large glasses.

Comfort yourself with a little pink milk at bedtime.

long tall raspberry and blueberry

200 g (7 oz) raspberries
200 g (7 oz) blueberries
500 ml (2 cups) milk

Chill 2 or 3 tall glasses in the freezer for 20 minutes. Blend the raspberries and blueberries in a blender until smooth. Pour about 60 ml (¼ cup) of the berry purée into a jug and carefully swirl in a spiral pattern around the inside of the glasses. Return to the freezer. Add the milk to the blender with the remaining berry purée and blend until thick and creamy. Pour into the glasses and serve. Makes 2 large glasses.

Note: Any berries are suitable for this drink. When in season, try mulberries. Depending on the sweetness of the berries, you may want to add a little honey. Even those with lactose intolerance can enjoy this drink — it is delicious made with rice milk.

Give 'em the old razzle-dazzle and watch 'em return for more.

razzle dazzle

1 lime
150 g (5½ oz) raspberries
1 teaspoon natural vanilla extract (essence)
200 g (7 oz) strawberry frozen yoghurt

Juice the lime in a citrus press. Blend the raspberries, lime juice, vanilla and frozen yoghurt in a blender until smooth. Makes 2 small glasses.

blue maple

Whip these up for the kids and you'll be the fairy godmother.

apple and blackcurrant shake

250 ml (1 cup) apple and blackcurrant juice
2 tablespoons natural yoghurt
185 ml (¾ cup) milk
3 scoops vanilla ice cream

Blend the juice, yoghurt, milk and ice cream in a blender until well combined and fluffy. Makes 2 medium glasses.

No one can be peachy keen all the time, so fake it in style.

peachy keen

2 large peaches, chopped
60 g (1/2 cup) raspberries
185 g (3/4 cup) low-fat peach and mango yoghurt
185 ml (3/4 cup) apricot nectar
8 large ice cubes
peach wedges, to serve

Blend the peaches, raspberries, yoghurt, apricot nectar and ice cubes in a blender until thick and smooth. Serve with the peach wedges. Makes 2 medium glasses.

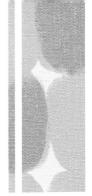

The ultimate classic combo, this version gives peaches and cream a modern makeover.

peach nectar spider fluff

600 ml (21 fl oz) peach nectar
600 ml (21 fl oz) soda water
4 scoops vanilla ice cream
1 peach, sliced

Combine the peach nectar and soda water in a jug. Pour into 4 tall glasses, top each with a scoop of ice cream and garnish with a slice of peach. Makes 4 medium glasses.

Just when winter thinks it's got you cornered, strike back with vitamin-rich, sweet dried fruit.

pear and peach protein drink

3 dried pear halves
3 dried peach halves
1 egg
2 tablespoons low-fat peach yoghurt
400 ml (14 fl oz) skim milk
1 tablespoon malted milk powder
1 tablespoon ground almonds
ground cinnamon, to serve

Put the pears, peaches and 125 ml (1/2 cup) boiling water into a heatproof bowl. Set aside for 10 minutes, or until the fruit is plump and juicy. Drain the fruit, reserving the soaking liquid, and allow to cool. Chop the fruit and blend with the soaking liquid, egg, yoghurt, milk, malted milk powder and almonds in a blender until thick and smooth. Serve sprinkled with a little cinnamon. Makes 2 medium glasses.

apple and blackcurrant shake

Let this mineral-rich smoothie work its magic on any wayward moods or blood sugar levels.

banana and berry vanilla smoothie

2 bananas, chopped
200 g (7 oz) mixed berries
3 tablespoons low-fat vanilla fromage frais or whipped yoghurt
500 ml (2 cups) skim milk
1 tablespoon oat bran

Blend the banana, berries, fromage frais, milk and oat bran in a blender for 2 minutes, or until thick and creamy. Makes 2 medium glasses.

Note: The smoothie will be thicker if you use frozen berries. You may need to add an extra 125 ml (1/2 cup) skim milk to thin it down.

Go low on fat but keep the full-on flavour with this mineral-rich revitalizer.

banana date smoothie

2 bananas, chopped
50 g (1/3 cup) fresh dates, pitted and chopped
250 g (1 cup) low-fat natural yoghurt
125 ml (1/2 cup) skim milk
8 ice cubes

Blend the banana, dates, yoghurt, milk and ice cubes in a blender until smooth. Makes 2 medium glasses.

We could all do with one of these!

good start to the day

2 bananas, chopped
1 large mango, chopped
500 ml (2 cups) skim milk
500 ml (2 cups) orange juice or pink grapefruit juice

Blend the banana, mango, milk and orange or pink grapefruit juice in a blender until smooth. Pour into a jug and chill. Makes 4 small glasses.

The sort of drink to make us go weak at the knees.

caramelized banana shake

2 bananas, chopped
500 ml (2 cups) milk
2 scoops ice cream
1½ tablespoons caramel sauce
1 tablespoon malted milk powder
pinch ground cinnamon

Blend the banana, milk, ice cream, caramel sauce, malted milk powder
and cinnamon in a blender until smooth. Makes 2 large glasses.

good start to the day

Pop the blueberry bubbles for a tongue-tingling explosion.

mango smoothie with fresh berries

2 mangoes, chopped
125 ml (1/2 cup) milk
250 ml (1 cup) buttermilk
1 tablespoon caster (superfine) sugar
2 scoops mango gelati or sorbet
50 g (1/3 cup) blueberries

Blend the mango, milk, buttermilk, sugar and gelati in a blender until smooth. Serve garnished with the blueberries. Makes 4 small glasses.

Blend away for a fresh and spicy blast.

spiced mango lassi

3 mangoes, chopped
250 g (1 cup) natural yoghurt
250 ml (1 cup) milk
1 teaspoon honey
1 teaspoon ground cinnamon
1/2 teaspoon ground cardamom

Blend the mango, yoghurt, milk, honey, cinnamon and cardamom in a blender until thick and smooth. Makes 2 medium glasses.

Note: Lassis are popular drinks in India where they are served alongside curries — the yoghurt cools and cleanses the palate. They can also be made with buttermilk.

Do the hippy hippy shake with a luscious mound of melon.

melon shake

1/2 small rockmelon (or other orange-fleshed melon), peeled,
  seeded and chopped
5 scoops vanilla ice cream
375 ml (1 1/2 cups) milk
2 tablespoons honey
ground nutmeg, to serve

Blend the rockmelon in a blender for 30 seconds, or until smooth. Add the
ice cream, milk and honey and blend for a further 10–20 seconds, or until
well combined and smooth. Serve sprinkled with ground nutmeg. Makes
2 medium glasses.

Light, juicy watermelon cuts through the creaminess of this indulgent blend. Making it all right. Right?

watermelon smoothie

600 g (3 cups) chopped watermelon
125 g (1/2 cup) yoghurt
250 ml (1 cup) milk
1 tablespoon caster (superfine) sugar
2 scoops vanilla ice cream

Blend the watermelon, yoghurt, milk and sugar in a blender until smooth. Add the ice cream and blend for a few seconds, or until frothy. Makes 4 small glasses.

Note: Use seedless watermelon if possible. Otherwise, pick out as many seeds as you can before blending.

watermelon smoothie

Start the day in a relaxed way with this vitamin-B-rich cocktail.

passionfruit breakfast shake

150 g (5¹/2 oz) passionfruit and other mixed fruit (mango, banana,
  peaches, strawberries, blueberries)
60 g (¹/4 cup) vanilla yoghurt
250 ml (1 cup) milk
2 teaspoons wheat germ
1 tablespoon honey
1 egg, optional
1 tablespoon malted milk powder

Blend the fruit, yoghurt, milk, wheat germ, honey, egg and malted milk
powder in a blender for 30–60 seconds, or until well combined. Makes
2 medium glasses.

Intense but smooth. It's kinda nice like that.

passionfruit and vanilla ice cream smoothie

170 g (6 oz) canned passionfruit pulp in syrup
140 ml (5 fl oz) can coconut milk
250 ml (1 cup) milk
25 g (¼ cup) desiccated coconut
¼ teaspoon natural vanilla extract (essence)
3 scoops vanilla ice cream

Blend half the passionfruit pulp, the coconut milk, milk, coconut, vanilla and ice cream in a blender until smooth and fluffy. Stir through the remaining passionfruit pulp. Makes 2 medium glasses.

Serve in a parfait glass with long spoons and curly straws for the genuine diner experience.

passionfruit and vanilla ice cream whip

4 passionfruit
100 g (3½ oz) passionfruit yoghurt
500 ml (2 cups) milk
1 tablespoon caster (superfine) sugar
2–4 scoops vanilla ice cream

Push the passionfruit pulp through a sieve to remove the seeds. Transfer to a blender with the yoghurt, milk, sugar and 2 scoops of ice cream and blend until smooth. Pour into 2 glasses and top each with an extra scoop of ice cream, if desired. Makes 2 medium glasses.

Finish this off with a generous dribble of homemade passionfruit syrup — and let it finish you off.

passionfruit ice cream soda

6 passionfruit
2¹/₂ cups (625 ml) lemonade
2–4 scoops vanilla ice cream

Combine the passionfruit pulp (you will need 125 ml/¹/₂ cup) with the lemonade, pour into 2 glasses and top each with 1–2 scoops of ice cream. Serve with straws and long spoons. Makes 2 large glasses.

passionfruit ice cream soda

Once you get started you may not be able to stop, so make sure there's plenty to go round.

blueberry starter

200 g (7 oz) blueberries
250 g (1 cup) natural yoghurt
250 ml (1 cup) milk
1 tablespoon wheat germ
1–2 teaspoons honey, to taste

Blend the blueberries, yoghurt, milk, wheat germ and honey in a blender until smooth. Makes 2 medium glasses.

Note: Frozen blueberries are great for this recipe. There is no need to thaw them before use.

A knockout serve, with berries for sweetener.

mixed berry protein punch

250 g (9 oz) mixed berries (strawberries, raspberries, blueberries)
1 tablespoon protein powder
200 g (7 oz) vanilla yoghurt
375 ml (1 1/2 cups) milk
2 tablespoons ground almonds

Blend the berries, protein powder, yoghurt, milk and ground almonds in
a blender until smooth. Makes 2 large glasses.

Discover the delights of the frozen fruit section and conjure up summer with this berry slushy.

cranberry, raspberry and vanilla slushy

500 ml (2 cups) cranberry juice
300 g (10½ oz) frozen raspberries
1 tablespoon caster (superfine) sugar
200 g (7 oz) vanilla yoghurt
about 10 ice cubes, crushed

Blend the cranberry juice, frozen raspberries, sugar, yoghurt and ice cubes in a blender until smooth. Makes 2 large glasses.

Note: To make your own vanilla yoghurt, simply scrape the seeds from a vanilla bean into a large tub of natural yoghurt, add the pod and refrigerate overnight.

School days were never this cool.

cranberry and vanilla ice cream spider

185 ml (3/4 cup) cream
1 tablespoon caster (superfine) sugar
500 ml (2 cups) cranberry juice
500 ml (2 cups) soda water
4 scoops vanilla ice cream
25 g (1/4 cup) flaked almonds, toasted

Whip the cream and sugar until soft peaks form. Combine the cranberry juice and soda water. Put a scoop of ice cream into 4 tall glasses. Pour the juice and soda over the ice cream. Spoon the whipped cream over and top with a sprinkle of almonds. Makes 4 medium glasses.

Tangy buttermilk adds protein and oomph to this low-fat fruity smoothie.

plum and prune tang

2 plums, stones removed and diced
150 g (1 cup) prunes, pitted and diced
250 g (1 cup) low-fat vanilla yoghurt
125 ml (1/2 cup) buttermilk
310 ml (1 1/4 cups) skim milk
8 large ice cubes

Blend the plums, prunes, yoghurt, buttermilk, milk and ice cubes in a blender until smooth. Makes 4 small glasses.

Figs are known as the fruit of love so serve this up for that someone special.

fig and ginger dream

6 small fresh figs
30 g (1 oz) ginger in syrup, plus 1 teaspoon syrup
625 ml (2¹/₂ cups) milk
2 teaspoons natural vanilla extract (essence)
ice cubes, to serve

Blend the figs, ginger, milk and vanilla in a blender until smooth. Serve over ice. Makes 2 large glasses.

cranberry, raspberry and vanilla slushy

One a berry, two a berry, three a berry, four.

berry yoghurt smoothie

250 g (9 oz) strawberries, hulled
125 g (4½ oz) frozen raspberries
250 g (1 cup) low-fat strawberry yoghurt
125 ml (½ cup) cranberry juice

Blend the strawberries, two-thirds of the frozen raspberries, the yoghurt and cranberry juice in a blender until smooth. Serve with a spoon, topped with the remaining raspberries. Makes 4 small glasses.

Too much strawberry is never enough.

summer strawberry smoothie

250 g (9 oz) strawberries, hulled
250 ml (1 cup) wildberry drinking yoghurt
4 scoops strawberry frozen yoghurt
1 tablespoon strawberry sauce
few drops natural vanilla extract (essence)
ice cubes, to serve

Blend the strawberries, yoghurt, frozen yoghurt, strawberry flavouring and vanilla in a blender until thick and smooth. Serve over ice. Makes 2 medium glasses.

Serve with buttermilk hotcakes for a truly impressive breakfast.

summer buttermilk smoothie

2 peaches
1/3 small rockmelon (or other orange-fleshed melon), peeled,
  seeded and chopped
150 g (5 1/2 oz) strawberries, hulled
4 mint leaves
125 ml (1/2 cup) buttermilk
125 ml (1/2 cup) orange juice
1–2 tablespoons honey

Cut a cross in the base of the peaches. Put them in a heatproof bowl and cover with boiling water. Leave for 1–2 minutes, then remove with a slotted spoon and plunge into cold water. Remove the skin and stones, and slice the flesh. Blend the peaches, rockmelon, strawberries and mint leaaves in a blender until smooth. Add the buttermilk, orange juice and 1 tablespoon of the honey and blend to combine. Taste for sweetness and add more honey if needed. Makes 2 medium glasses.

Frozen berries make the grade in all well-stocked freezers.

fruitasia smoothie

2 bananas, chopped
6 strawberries, hulled
100 g (3 1/2 oz) frozen raspberries
2 passionfruit
100 g (3 1/2 oz) 99.8% fat-free natural yoghurt
250 ml (1 cup) apple juice
2 ice cubes

Blend the banana, strawberries, frozen raspberries, passionfruit pulp, yoghurt, apple juice and ice cubes in a blender until smooth. Makes 4 small glasses.

summer strawberry smoothie

Use a light floral honey to avoid overwhelming the delicate flavour of the custard apple.

custard apple smoothie

2 custard apples, peeled and seeded
500 ml (2 cups) milk
2 teaspoons honey
1½ teaspoons natural vanilla extract (essence)
1 teaspoon rosewater
ice cubes, to serve

Blend the custard apple flesh, milk, honey, vanilla and rosewater in a blender until smooth. Serve over ice. Makes 2 large glasses.

Establish a new tradition at Christmas with this peachy take on an old classic.

peachy egg nog

2 eggs, separated
60 ml (¼ cup) milk
55 g (¼ cup) caster (superfine) sugar
80 ml (⅓ cup) cream
440 ml (1¾ cups) peach nectar
2 tablespoons orange juice
ground nutmeg, to garnish

Beat the egg yolks, milk and half the sugar in a bowl. Put the bowl over a pan of simmering water — do not allow the base of the bowl to touch the water. Cook, stirring, for 8 minutes, or until the custard thickens. Remove from the heat, cover the surface with plastic wrap and set aside to cool. Beat the egg whites until frothy. Add the remaining sugar, to taste, then beat until stiff peaks form. In a separate bowl, whip the cream until soft peaks form. Gently fold the egg whites and cream into the cooled custard. Stir through the peach nectar and orange juice. Cover and chill for 2 hours. Beat the mixture lightly. Serve sprinkled with nutmeg. Makes 4 small glasses.

Save a glass for the bath and soak your way to silky skin.

apricot and bran breakfast

100 g (3½ oz) dried apricots
1 tablespoon oat bran
60 g (¼ cup) apricot yoghurt
600 ml (21 fl oz) milk
1 tablespoon honey

Soak the dried apricots in boiling water until they are plump and
rehydrated, then drain. Blend the apricots, bran, yoghurt, milk and honey
in a blender until thick and smooth. Makes 2 large glasses.

Apricots whip up a little potent power pack.

apricot whip

75 g (2¹/₂ oz) dried apricots
125 g (¹/₂ cup) apricot yoghurt
170 ml (²/₃ cup) light coconut milk
310 ml (1¹/₄ cups) milk
1 scoop vanilla ice cream
1 tablespoon honey
flaked coconut, toasted, to garnish

Soak the dried apricots in boiling water for 15 minutes, then drain and roughly chop. Blend the apricots, yoghurt, coconut milk, milk, ice cream and honey in a blender until smooth. Serve sprinkled with the flaked coconut. Makes 2 medium glasses.

peachy egg nog

Indulge a passion for bananas with this filling thick-shake.

banana passion

3 passionfruit
1 large banana, chopped
60 g (¼ cup) low-fat natural yoghurt
250 ml (1 cup) skim milk

Blend the passionfruit pulp, banana, yoghurt and milk in a blender in short bursts until smooth and the seeds are finely chopped. (Add more milk if it is too thick.) Don't blend for too long or it will become very bubbly and increase in volume. Makes 2 small glasses.

Sweet, smooth and a little bit nutty — hmmm, sounds like an average day in the office.

banana sesame bender

3 small bananas, chopped
750 ml (3 cups) milk
1 1/2 tablespoons tahini
1 1/2 tablespoons peanut butter
1 tablespoon honey
2 teaspoons natural vanilla extract (essence)

Blend the banana, milk, tahini, peanut butter, honey and vanilla in a blender until smooth. Makes 2 large glasses.

If things have been a little on the turbulent side, save the day with potassium-rich banana.

banana, kiwi and mint smoothie

2 bananas, chopped
2 kiwifruit, peeled and chopped
5 g (¼ cup) mint leaves
250 ml (1 cup) milk or coconut milk
2 scoops vanilla ice cream

Blend the banana, kiwifruit, mint, milk and ice cream in a blender until smooth. Makes 2 medium glasses.

Make peace with your sweet tooth and indulge in a standing banana split.

creamy rich banana and macadamia smoothie

2 very ripe bananas, slightly frozen
100 g (3½ oz) honey-roasted macadamias
2 tablespoons vanilla honey yoghurt
500 ml (2 cups) milk
2 tablespoons wheat germ
1 banana, extra, halved lengthways

Blend the frozen bananas, 60 g (2¼ oz) of the macadamias, the yoghurt, milk and wheat germ in a blender for several minutes until thick and creamy. Finely chop the remaining macadamias and put on a plate. Toss the banana halves in the nuts to coat. Stand a banana half in each glass or stand on the glass edge. Pour in the smoothie. Makes 2 large glasses.

Note: The bananas need to be very ripe. Peel and chop them, toss in lemon juice and freeze in an airtight container ready for use later on.

creamy rich banana and macadamia smoothie

Get to know your papayas in the best way possible.

papaya and orange smoothie

1 papaya, peeled, seeded and chopped
1 orange, peeled and chopped
6–8 ice cubes
200 g (7 oz) natural yoghurt
1–2 tablespoons caster (superfine) sugar
ground nutmeg, to serve

Blend the papaya, orange and ice cubes in a blender until smooth. Add the yoghurt and blend to combine. Add the sugar, to taste. Serve sprinkled with nutmeg. Makes 2 medium glasses.

Note: This keeps well for 6 hours in the fridge. Peach or apricot flavoured yoghurt may be used for added flavour.

Why mess with a classic?

coconut and lime lassi

400 ml (14 fl oz) coconut milk
185 g (3/4 cup) natural yoghurt
60 ml (1/4 cup) lime juice
55 g (1/4 cup) caster (superfine) sugar
8–10 ice cubes
lime slices, to garnish

Blend the coconut milk, yoghurt, lime juice, sugar and ice cubes in a blender until well combined and smooth. Serve garnished with lime slices. Makes 2 medium glasses.

Note: Use strong, creamy yoghurt to make sure the lassi has tang.

The avocado, master of disguise, is of course a fruit — and one that packs a protein punch.

avocado smoothie

1 small avocado, peeled, stone removed
500 ml (2 cups) milk
3 teaspoons honey
1/2 teaspoon natural vanilla extract (essence)

Blend the avocado, milk, honey and vanilla in a blender until smooth. Makes 2 medium glasses.

Don't judge a book by its cover, this Latin smoothie is a serious heartbreaker.

latin smoothie

1 small avocado, peeled, stone removed
125 ml (1/2 cup) condensed milk
juice of 1 lime
1 teaspoon natural vanilla extract (essence)
8 large ice cubes

Blend the avocado, condensed milk, lime juice, vanilla, ice cubes and 250 ml (1 cup) water in a blender until smooth. Makes 2 medium glasses.

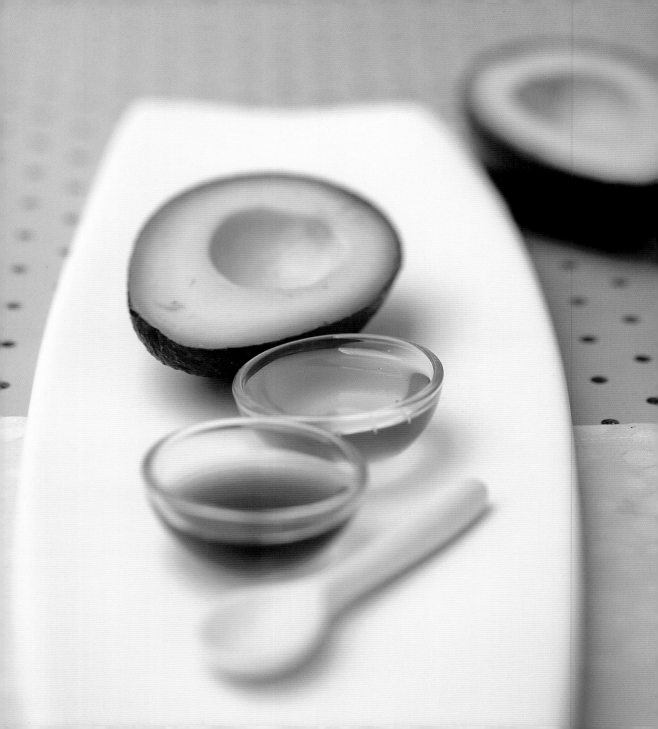

avocado smoothie

Good prepared custard is readily available these days so feel free to take the easy road to sweetie heaven.

cinnamon and custard shake

375 ml (1 1/2 cups) milk
185 ml (3/4 cup) prepared custard
3 scoops vanilla ice cream
3 teaspoons honey
1 1/2 teaspoons ground cinnamon
ground cinnamon, extra, to serve

Blend the milk, custard, ice cream, honey and cinnamon until smooth and fluffy. Serve sprinkled with extra cinnamon. Makes 2 medium glasses.

374

A hot, creamy drink at bedtime is one of the few pleasures that lasts a lifetime.

creamy almond and vanilla shake

1 vanilla bean, halved lengthways
500 ml (2 cups) milk
80 g (1/2 cup) raw almonds, toasted
1 tablespoon pure maple syrup
1 teaspoon almond extract (essence)

Put the vanilla bean and milk into a saucepan and heat until almost boiling. Remove from the heat and set aside to infuse for 5 minutes. Return the pan to the heat and heat again until almost boiling. Remove the vanilla bean. Blend the milk, almonds, maple syrup and almond extract in a blender until thick and smooth. Makes 2 medium glasses.

Note: You can rinse the vanilla bean, let it dry and put it in an airtight container of caster (superfine) sugar. Use this vanilla sugar to flavour the drink in place of the maple syrup.

Add a plate of shortbread and a bowl of whipped cream for a pared-down take on the real thing.

vanilla apple pie

3 apples or 250 ml (1 cup) bottled apple juice
200 g (7 oz) canned pie apple
2 scoops vanilla ice cream
1/2 teaspoon ground cinnamon
1 teaspoon natural vanilla extract (essence)
ground cinnamon or freshly grated nutmeg, to serve, optional

Juice the apples through a juice extractor. Blend the apple juice, pie apple, ice cream, cinnamon and vanilla in a blender until smooth. Serve sprinkled with cinnamon or nutmeg, if desired. Makes 2 medium glasses.

Delight your inner child, or even a real one, with this modern take on an old favourite.

apricot crumble smoothie

200 g (7 oz) canned apricots in natural juice
200 g (7 oz) vanilla yoghurt
250 ml (1 cup) milk
1 tablespoon wheat germ
1 tablespoon malted milk powder
large pinch ground cinnamon

Blend the undrained apricots, yoghurt, milk, wheat germ, malted milk powder and cinnamon in a blender until smooth. Makes 2 large glasses.

Note: Canned peaches, apples or pears can be used instead of apricots.

apricot crumble smoothie

other ways to be a smoothie Take the road less travelled, the path little beaten, the track grown over with infrequent use. No longer do you need to look longingly at the dairy blends and think, if only

I could — you can! For among coconut and almond milk, tofu and soy milk you have friends stout of heart and firm of flavour. Know truly that dairy milk and its ilk don't necessarily rule the smoothie waves.

A lactose-free option, almond milk is not much thicker than milk, but its flavour is highly distinctive — similar to that of marzipan. It goes well with fruit such as dates, grapes, peaches and strawberries, and is available from health food stores and Italian delicatessens. Do not buy almond milk syrup, as it is very different. Fresh coconut milk from whole coconuts sounds impressive but, let's be honest, the canned variety is a tad easier to get at. Coconut cream produces drinks with a better consistency than coconut milk does, but is higher in fat. With both, buy good-quality brands to ensure milk with a lovely white colour. Light coconut milk can also be used; it has a thinner consistency. Blend with tropical fruit, raspberries and cherries. silken tofu may seem a strange inclusion here, but its textural qualities and nutritional benefits make it a welcome one. Its smoothie partners are tropical fruits such as banana and mango. Unlike cow's or goat's milk, soy milk does not contain lactose sugar or cholesterol. It has antioxidant benefits, but little calcium, so buy calcium-fortified soy milk if you're using it in place of dairy products. Soy milk can be quite sweet, so taste before adding other sweeteners such as honey. Use with warm flavours such as pears, cinnamon, dates and apricots. Soy yoghurt and soy ice cream are also good choices. extras: carob powder is sweet and has a similar flavour to chocolate, but without the fat. Lecithin meal is a natural soy-derived nutritional supplement, and its reputed properties range from aiding the liver to improving memory. Buy both from health food stores.

Smooth, thick and calming, consider using any leftovers as a fragrant facial!

almond, papaya and date shake

1/2 papaya, peeled, seeded and chopped
4 fresh dates, pitted and chopped
375 ml (1 1/2 cups) almond milk
1 teaspoon rosewater
ice cubes, to serve

Blend the papaya, dates, almond milk and rosewater in a blender until smooth. Serve over ice. Makes 2 medium glasses.

Almond milk is special-occasion material in the Middle East but don't let that stop you from making this as often as you want.

almond and grape frappé

500 g (1 lb 2 oz) green seedless grapes
250 ml (1 cup) almond milk
large pinch ground cinnamon
8 large ice cubes

Juice the grapes through a juice extractor. Blend the grape juice, almond milk, cinnamon and ice cubes in a blender until smooth. Makes 2 medium glasses.

Note: Almonds are high in calcium and an excellent inclusion in a dairy-free diet.

A veritable bazaar of flavours — sweet, nutty and smooth as a bolt of silk.

whipped nougat

200 g (1 cup) canned apricots in natural juice
500 ml (2 cups) almond milk
1 1/2 teaspoons natural vanilla extract (essence)
1 teaspoon honey
few drops rosewater, optional
8 large ice cubes

Blend the undrained apricots, almond milk, vanilla, honey, rosewater and ice cubes in a blender until smooth. Makes 2 large glasses.

Cherries seem so indulgent — this drink will do nothing to change that impression.

almond cherry smoothie

375 ml (1 1/2 cups) almond milk
400 g (14 oz) cherries, pitted
1/4 teaspoon natural vanilla extract (essence)
pinch ground cinnamon
4 large ice cubes

Blend the almond milk, cherries, vanilla, cinnamon and ice cubes in a blender until smooth. Makes 2 large glasses.

Note: If you like a strong almond or marzipan flavour, add a dash of almond extract (essence).

almond cherry smoothie

This one takes us back to our trampoline days (without having to do the actual bouncing).

coconut cream and raspberry shake

300 g (10¹/₂ oz) raspberries
250 ml (1 cup) apple and blackcurrant juice
400 ml (14 fl oz) coconut cream
2 scoops vanilla soy ice cream
marshmallows, to serve

Blend the raspberries, apple and blackcurrant juice, coconut cream and ice cream in a blender for several minutes until thick and creamy. Thread marshmallows onto 4 swizzle sticks and serve with the shakes, along with a straw and a long spoon. Makes 4 small glasses.

Note: For a low-fat drink, blend the raspberries and juice with ice instead of coconut cream and ice cream.

Okay, so this is not one for the dieters, but that's just the way it is sometimes.

cherrycoco

400 g (14 oz) cherries, pitted
400 ml (14 fl oz) coconut milk
2 teaspoons caster (superfine) sugar
1 teaspoon natural vanilla extract (essence)
ice cubes, to serve

Juice the cherries though a juice extractor. Shake well with the coconut milk, sugar and vanilla. Serve over ice. Makes 2 small glasses.

Note: You could use vanilla sugar in this recipe — just keep a vanilla bean in a jar of sugar for fragrant sugar.

Papa don't preach, I'm taking good care of myself with a healthy dose of papaya.

coconut and papaya frappé

1/2 papaya, peeled, seeded and chopped
400 ml (14 fl oz) coconut milk
2 tablespoons lime juice
2 tablespoons caster (superfine) sugar
1 teaspoon natural vanilla extract (essence)
pinch allspice
8 large ice cubes

Blend the payaya, coconut milk, lime juice, sugar, vanilla, allspice and ice cubes in a blender until smooth. Makes 2 large glasses.

I've got a lovely bunch of coconuts so let's make some ice, ice, baby.

coconut and lime ice

400 ml (14 fl oz) coconut milk
juice of 4 limes
2 teaspoons natural vanilla extract (essence)
80 g (1/3 cup) caster (superfine) sugar
7 g (1/3 cup) mint leaves, optional
8 large ice cubes

Blend the coconut milk, lime juice, vanilla, sugar, mint and ice cubes in a blender until smooth. Makes 2 large glasses.

coconut cream and raspberry shake

When the island breeze is calling but work has you stalling, take an instant holiday with this tropical shake.

coconut and mango shake

400 g (14 oz) fresh mango pulp
125 ml (1/2 cup) lime juice
125 ml (1/2 cup) coconut milk
2 teaspoons honey
3 teaspoons finely chopped mint
12 large ice cubes

Blend the mango pulp, lime juice, coconut milk, honey, mint and ice cubes in a blender until thick and smooth. Chill well. Stir to combine. Makes 2 medium glasses.

Go the whole hog and serve this in cocktail glasses with lychees on toothpicks. And perhaps a splash of white rum.

pineapple and lychee creamy colada

1/3 pineapple, peeled and chopped
750 ml (3 cups) pineapple juice
500 g (1 lb 2 oz) canned lychees
2 tablespoons spearmint leaves
125 ml (1/2 cup) coconut cream
crushed ice

Blend the pineapple, pineapple juice, lychees and their juice and spearmint in a blender until smooth. Add the coconut cream and crushed ice and blend until thick and smooth. Makes 6 medium glasses.

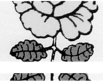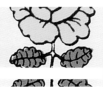

If you've been good, reward yourself by using coconut cream for an extra luscious tipple.

island blend

1/3 pineapple, peeled and chopped
1/2 small papaya, peeled, seeded and chopped
2 small bananas, chopped
60 ml (1/4 cup) coconut milk
250 ml (1 cup) orange juice
ice cubes, to serve

Blend the pineapple, papaya, banana and coconut milk in a blender until smooth. Add the orange juice and blend until combined. Serve over ice. Makes 2 medium glasses.

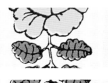

For a kitsch centrepiece, serve this in a hollowed-out pineapple.

coconut and pineapple iced drink

1 pineapple, peeled
250 ml (1 cup) coconut milk
mint leaves, to garnish
pineapple leaves, to garnish

Juice the pineapple through a juice extractor. Stir through the coconut milk in a large jug. Pour 125 ml (1/2 cup) of the mixture into 8 holes of an ice-cube tray and freeze. Chill the remaining mixture. When the ice cubes have frozen, pour the juice mixture into 2 glasses, add the ice cubes and garnish with mint and pineapple leaves. Makes 2 medium glasses.

pineapple and lychee creamy colada

Ascend to berry yoghurt heaven with a clear conscience.

strawberry lassi

250 g (9 oz) strawberries, hulled
300 g (10½ oz) strawberry soy yoghurt
2 tablespoons honey
4 ice cubes

Blend the strawberries, yoghurt, honey, ice cubes and 2½ tablespoons water in a blender until smooth. Garnish with any leftover strawberries. Makes 2 small glasses.

This drink is musky and full of promise, with gentle warmth.

spiced melon shake

1/4 teaspoon cardamom seeds
350 ml (12 fl oz) creamy soy milk
1/2 rockmelon (or other orange-fleshed melon), peeled, seeded
  and chopped
1 tablespoon honey
2 tablespoons ground almonds
4 ice cubes

Lightly crush the cardamom seeds in a mortar and pestle or with the back
of a knife. Blend the cardamom and soy milk in a blender for 30 seconds.
Strain the soy milk and rinse any remaining seeds from the blender. Return
the strained milk to the blender, add the rockmelon, honey, almonds and
ice cubes and blend until smooth. Makes 2 medium glasses.

Buy these summer fruits by the tray and develop a smoothie habit you won't need to kick.

apricot tofu smoothie

4 apricots, stones removed
2 peaches, stones removed
250 ml (1 cup) apricot nectar
150 g (5¹/₂ oz) silken tofu

Blend the apricots, peaches, apricot nectar and tofu in a blender until smooth. Makes 2 medium glasses.

No corny jokes about soy good for you — one mouthful and you'll know it's true.

fresh date and pear soy shake

400 ml (14 fl oz) creamy soy milk
4 fresh dates, pitted and chopped
2 small pears, peeled, cored and chopped

Blend the soy milk, dates and pears in a blender until smooth. Makes 2 medium glasses.

strawberry lassi

Not a roadside attraction, just an ideal way to start the day.

big bold banana

750 ml (3 cups) soy milk
125 g (4¹/₂ oz) silken tofu
4 very ripe bananas, chopped
1 tablespoon honey
1 tablespoon natural vanilla extract (essence)
1 tablespoon carob powder (see Note)

Blend the soy milk, tofu, banana, honey, vanilla and carob powder in a blender until smooth. Serve with long spoons. Makes 4 medium glasses.

Note: Carob powder is available from health-food stores.

Coffee and breakfast in one easy package.

banana soy latte

440 ml (1¾ cups) coffee-flavoured soy milk
2 bananas, chopped
8 large ice cubes
1 teaspoon drinking chocolate
¼ teaspoon ground cinnamon

Blend the soy milk and banana in a blender until smooth. With the blender running, add the ice cubes one at a time until well incorporated. Serve sprinkled with the drinking chocolate and ground cinnamon. Makes 4 small glasses.

If the Aloha evening breeze swept you away, rest and repair the morning after.

tropical morning soy smoothie

2 mangoes, chopped
350 ml (12 fl oz) creamy soy milk
150 ml (5½ fl oz) pineapple juice
15 g (¼ cup) chopped mint
6 ice cubes
mint sprigs, to garnish

Blend the mango, soy milk, pineapple juice, mint and ice cubes in a blender until smooth. Serve garnished with mint. Makes 2 large glasses.

Keep mum happy and make this breakfast-in-a-glass part of your routine.

get up and go smoothie

1/2 mango, chopped
60 g (1/4 cup) vanilla soy yoghurt
500 ml (2 cups) no-fat soy milk
2 tablespoons oat bran
2 tablespoons honey

Blend the mango, yoghurt, soy milk, oat bran and honey in a blender until smooth. Serve with spoons. Makes 4 small glasses.

banana soy latte

Breakfast is the most important meal of the day but there is no reason why it shouldn't also be the yummiest.

maple banana breakfast

350 ml (12 fl oz) fresh or creamy soy milk
150 g (5½ oz) vanilla soy yoghurt
2 very ripe bananas, chopped
1 large yellow peach, chopped
2 teaspoons lecithin meal
2 tablespoons maple syrup

Blend the soy milk, yoghurt, banana, peach, lecithin meal and maple syrup in a blender until smooth. Makes 2 medium glasses.

Fill a thermos for an emergency breakfast on the run that really works.

wheaty starter

2 breakfast wheat biscuits
2 bananas, chopped
60 g (¼ cup) vanilla soy yoghurt
500 ml (2 cups) no-fat soy milk

Blend the wheat biscuits, banana, yoghurt and soy milk in a blender until smooth. Makes 4 small glasses.

Don't throw away black, spotted bananas, their lush ripeness is the highlight of this smoothie.

carob peanut smoothie

400 ml (14 oz) carob- or chocolate-flavoured soy milk
2 very ripe bananas, chopped
150 g (5½ oz) silken tofu
2 tablespoons honey
1 tablespoon peanut butter

Blend the soy milk, banana, tofu, honey and peanut butter in a blender until smooth. Makes 2 medium or 4 small glasses.

Strong, sweet and powerful — a real super hero!

peanut choc power smoothie

500 ml (2 cups) chocolate-flavoured soy milk
125 g (4½ oz) silken tofu
60 g (¼ cup) peanut butter
2 bananas, chopped
2 tablespoons chocolate sauce
8 large ice cubes

Blend the soy milk, tofu, peanut butter, banana, chocolate syrup and ice cubes in a blender until smooth. Makes 4 small glasses.

carob peanut smoothie

index

421

422

423

424

425

432